Landscapes of

LA GOMERA
and
SOUTHERN TENERIFE

a countryside guide
Eighth edition

Noel Rochford
revised by *Sunflower* Books

SUNFLOWER BOOKS

Eighth edition © 2018
Sunflower Books™
PO Box 36160
London SW7 3WS, UK
www.sunflowerbooks.co.uk

ISBN 978-1-85691-504-5

Aeonium at Pavon

Important note to the reader

We have tried to ensure that the descriptions and maps in this book are error-free at press date. The book will be updated, where necessary, whenever future printings permit. It will be very helpful for us to receive your comments (sent to info@sunflowerbooks.co.uk, please) for the updating of future printings.

   We also rely on those who use this book — especially walkers — to take along a good supply of common sense when they explore. Conditions change fairly rapidly in the Canary Islands, and *storm damage or bulldozing may make a route unsafe at any time*. If the route is not as we outline it here, and your way ahead is not secure, return to the point of departure! *Never attempt to complete a tour or walk under hazardous conditions!* Please read carefully the notes on pages 32-41 and the introductory comments at the beginning of each tour and walk (regarding road conditions, equipment, grade, distances and time, etc). Explore *safely*, while at the same time respecting the beauty of the countryside.

Cover photograph: Roque Carmona and El Teide from the GR 131
Title page: Sign at Taguluche's chapel (Ermita Virgen del Buen Viaje)

Photographs: the author and Sunflower Books, except for page 60: Andreas Stieglitz; 64 (top right), 66 (bottom), 72-3, 79, 94, 107 (bottom), 116 (bottom), 119, 129, 136: Conny Spelbrink; 2, 7, 14, 25, 29 (bottom), 66 (top), 75, 76, 87 (middle), 92, 111, 112-3, 114 (bottom): Robert Lefever; 13, 20 (bottom), 26, 43, 47, 62, 64 (bottom left), 87 (bottom) and cover: Shutterstock
Drawings: Sharon Rochford
Maps: Nick Hill for Sunflower Books. Base map data © OpenStreetMap contributors. Contour data made available under ODbL (opendata commons.org/licenses/odbl/1.0)
Printed and bound in England: Short Run Press, Exeter

Contents

4 Landscapes of La Gomera and southern Tenerife

Preface

Few places in the world can offer the kaleidoscope of natural beauty found in the Canary Islands. What one island lacks, another has in plenty. Each island has a personality of its own — as you will see if you use this book to explore *both* La Gomera and Tenerife.

Over the years, people have asked me why this book is not devoted *solely* to La Gomera (admittedly, my favourite Canary Island). The reason is simple: since there are no direct flights from the UK or northern Europe to the island, most people fly to Reina Sofía airport in the south of Tenerife and go on to Gomera by ferry from the nearby port at Los Cristianos. So if you are going via Tenerife anyway, why not spend some time there and see the best of it? That's the way this book is presented — starting with introductory tours and walks on Tenerife, the guide moves on to explore La Gomera in depth.

The south of Tenerife is associated with bodies and beaches. Few visitors explore beyond the 'compulsory' coach tour to El Teide. They may return home thinking of Tenerife's landscape as barren, however magnificent. They have missed the laurel forests of the Anaga and the soft green valleys of the Teno Peninsula. The car tours described in this book put the *entire island* within easy reach. *Do* get out and explore — you'll be surprised! You may even be enticed to return and get to know the whole island in depth. If so, my companion guide, *Landscapes of Tenerife* (also published by Sunflower) will put both long and short walks in the Teno and Anaga peninsulas, La Orotava and Las Cañadas at your fingertips.

Few people think of walking in the south of Tenerife because the bleached façade of the interior looks rather unappealing from the coast, and in summer it can be very hot and sunny. But during the winter months some days will be cool and ideal for walking. The nine walks described here — two of them (Paisaje Lunar and Masca) among Tenerife's top walks, the other seven less well known — lead to exhilarating beauty spots. You'll venture upon canyon-sized ravines, gorges overflowing with vegetation, waterfalls and trickling streams — all well concealed in this supposedly 'bleak' landscape. These walks have been chosen for their easy access from the south.

When you've explored a bit on Tenerife, move on to La Gomera. Tantalizingly close, this little dome-shaped island sits some 20 miles southwest of Los Cristianos — just 50 minutes away by high-speed ferry. The ferry schedules allow you enough time to go even for one day's touring or walking — but I recommend *at least* a week.

La Gomera is a total contrast to the *playas* of southern Tenerife. It's a place where people go to appreciate the simple things in life — peace and quiet, space to breathe and splendid rural scenery. In all three of these it excels, and, on top of this, the island remains largely unspoilt.

La Gomera is a walkers' paradise. But if you're not a walker, explore the island by car. Break up your tours with leg-stretching breaks to visit some of my favourite picnic spots (see page 8). Many of these picnic settings lie along the route of a long walk, so you can get the 'feel' of the landscape without hiking for miles. Perhaps, unawares, you will find yourself drawn deeper and deeper into the countryside.

Getting to know an island is getting to know the people, so before you set off, learn a few words of Spanish. The 'Gomeros' are a reserved people. However, if you do speak some Spanish, you will find them responsive and helpful. (It's not likely that you'll have time to master the other 'language' spoken on La Gomera — the *silbo,* a centuries-old 'whistling language' developed by the Guanches to communicate across the enormous ravines that slice down from the *cumbre*.)

Whether you are exploring Tenerife, La Gomera, or both islands, this book should help you to find somewhere enchanting, taste something unusual, and meet like-minded people — the essence, I hope, of a memorable visit.

Acknowledgements

My special thanks to Conny Spelbrink, who rewalked *all* the routes for the Sixth edition in 2014 and to my publishers, who thoroughly revised this Eighth edition on the ground immediately prior to publication.

Useful books

There are several general guides devoted to Tenerife, but nothing in English for La Gomera — so it's probably best to choose a guide to all the Canary Islands from your favourite travel series. *Do* try to buy a copy of *Wild flowers of the Canary Islands* by David and Zoe Bramwell on the web before travelling.

Also available: Landscapes of Tenerife (Teno • Orotava • Anaga • Cañadas), Landscapes of Gran Canaria, Landscapes of Lanzarote, Landscapes of Fuerteventura, Landscapes of La Palma and El Hierro. All by Noel Rochford and published by Sunflower Books.

Getting about

Tenerife

The best way to get around the island is by **hiring a car** (or motorbike). **Coach tours** are also a popular way of seeing Tenerife. While **taxis** cater for those with less time and more money, sharing can make them worthwhile.

If you're not pushed for time, the local **buses run by Titsa (www.titsa.com)** are fun and inexpensive — invest in fare-saving travel cards, valid on the tram and all bus lines except 342 and 348 to Teide. The plan on the touring map inside the back cover shows bus stations and some major stops in the southern tourist centres. The bus network is very extensive, but if you're going far from your base in the south, schedules may not permit you to take *long* walks: you may need to arrange alternative transport.

La Gomera

If you only spend a day or two, a **hire car** is the best way of getting about. If you're visiting from Tenerife, you can either take your car over or hire a car in San Sebastián (near the port or in town). If you're going straight to Gomera, it should be cheaper to arrange car hire at home before you travel. **Coach tours** and **taxis** are other options of course.

Local **buses (www.guaguagomera.com)** service the ferry arrivals/departures. Morning buses bring passengers from around the island for the first departure, return to the villages with arrivals, head back to the port, etc. Together with the **passenger ferry (www.fredolsen.es)** mentioned on page 141 most walks can be reached without a car.

Approaching Cruce de la Zarcita on the GM2, with views to Roque Carmona in the foreground and El Teide on Tenerife in the distance

☀ Picnicking

Picnickers are extremely well catered for on both Tenerife and La Gomera. The authorities have set up several well-equipped 'recreation areas' around the islands. All have been laid out in harmony with their surroundings. At these *zonas recreativas* (which tend to be crowded on weekends and holidays), you'll find tables, benches and drinking fountains. Many are also equipped with barbecues, WCs and play areas for children. All **roadside** picnic areas **with tables** (and sometimes other facilities) are indicated in the touring notes and on the touring maps by the symbol ⋝.

I've also included some other ideas for motorists. Sometimes during a walk I've come upon a terrific view or pretty setting not far off the car touring road. If so, I've used the symbol ℗ both in the car touring text and on the touring map to alert you to it. If it is some way from the roadside and involves a short walk, then look for the same symbol on the large-scale *walking* map for the area to find out *exactly* where it is and how to get there. Obviously on Tenerife there are many appealing picnic spots not mentioned in the car tours, since this guide only includes walking maps for the south, so it wouldn't be possible to pinpoint their locations.

Two hints: Do park *well off* the road, so as not to inconvenience other motorists or the local people. And please heed the Country code on page 38 and go quietly in the countryside.

Walkers are spoilt for choice, of course. Look at this lovely setting in the Barranco de Guarimiar early on in Walk 26, with palms for shade and rocks to sit on.

Touring

Most people holidaying on Tenerife and Gomera hire a car for some part of their stay. It's very easy to travel between the islands — just 50 minutes by fast ferry (see timetables on page 141).

The four relatively long tours described here will get you well acquainted with **Tenerife**. If your time is limited, **Tour 1 is a must**, with **Tour 4** making a good follow-up.

There are two itineraries for **La Gomera**: I've simply split the island north/south. Should you only be visiting Gomera for one day, you can combine the two tours, *if you make a very early start* by fast ferry from Los Cristianos. If you're spending more time on Gomera and you're hiring a 4WD vehicle, you may find it helpful to look at the *walking maps* when touring, since only a few *tracks* are shown on the touring map.

The touring notes are brief: they contain little history or information readily available in leaflets freely available from the tourist offices. The facilities and 'sights' of the main towns are not described either, for the same reason. Instead, I concentrate on the 'logistics' of touring: times and distances, road conditions, and seeing places many tourists miss. Most of all, I emphasise possibilities for **walking** and **picnicking**. While a few of the references to picnics 'off the beaten track' (indicated by the symbol **P** in the touring notes) may not be suitable during a long car tour, you may see a landscape that you would like to explore at leisure another day.

The large fold-out touring maps are designed to be held out opposite the touring notes and contain all the information you will need outside the towns. The tours have been written up starting from Playa de las Américas (Tenerife) and Valle Gran Rey (La Gomera), but they can be joined from other points quite easily. Town plans are on the touring map.

Remember to allow plenty of time for **visits**, and to take along **warm clothing** as well as some **food and drink**, in case you are delayed. The distances quoted in the notes are *cumulative* from the departure point. A key to the symbols is on the touring maps.

All motorists should read the Country code on page 38. *Buen viaje!*

Car tour 1: LAS CAÑADAS AND THE NORTHWEST

Playa de las Américas • Vilaflor • Las Cañadas • La Orotava • Puerto de la Cruz • Icod de los Vinos • Buenavista • Punta de Teno • Masca • Santiago del Teide • Los Gigantes • San Juan • Playa de las Américas

240km/149mi; 8-9 hours' driving; Exit A from Playa de las Américas (plan on reverse of touring map)
En route: ⊼ at La Caldera, Las Lajas, Las Cañadas, Los Pedregales; Picnics (Ⓟ symbol on the touring and walking maps) Ifonche road, Boca Tauce, Piedras Amarillas, Masca, Araza; Walks 1, 2, (3-5), 6-8. (Other walks and picnic spots are described in *Landscapes of Tenerife*.) *This excursion requires a very early start. You may set off in sunshine, but the north is often under cloud. Less experienced motorists may find*

the road between Santiago and Masca unnerving. **Important:** *the road to Punta de Teno is only open Mon-Wed (see page 13); it is also dangerous in heavy rain and strong winds, due to rockfall. Puerto, La Orotava and Adeje (Walk 3) are best kept for another day; they are easily reached by bus or motorway. No petrol stations en route between Vilaflor and La Orotava!*
Opening hours: Aguamansa trout farm: 10.00-15.00 Mon-Sat; **Botanical Garden, Puerto de la Cruz:** 09.00-19.00 daily (18.00 in winter)

This dramatic circuit begins on the dry rocky slopes of the south. Ascending to Las Cañadas, you head up through a forest of Canary pines — the most beautiful you'll ever see. Las Cañadas is another world; you will cross a vast bare plateau, where rich volcanic hues ooze out of the landscape, and fields of jagged scoria and sunken gravel 'lakes' (*cañadas*) surround you. The north then greets you with the greenery of garden plots and trees; the lush Orotava Valley is a sea of rippling banana palms. Exhilarating coastal scenery takes you to the northwest and its concealed valleys. From gentle, scooped-out basins, you will plunge into precipitous, fathomless ravines.

Guajara rises on the eastern edge of the Cañadas; it's near the starting point for Walks 7c and d, but also a prominent, if distant, feature on Walk 6.

Head east along either the motorway or the TF481 just to the south of it, and at Exit 72 turn off right for 'EL TEIDE'. You join the TF28 and pass the **Camel Park** (★). Some 4.5km uphill, turn left on the TF51, passing a road to **Las Aguilas Jungle Park**★. You climb through a bleak landscape. Cacti and *tabaiba* flourish in this rocky terrain, and mock pepper trees grow alongside the road. Come into **Arona** (11km 🛉🍽🏨), a village with a charming shady church square, surrounded by balconied old houses. A short drive leads to El Vento where Walk 2 starts and ends. Further uphill, just before **La Escalona**, the road left to Ifonche (🅿) would take you to parking for Walks 4 and 5.

Hillocks of all shapes and sizes disrupt the plains. Continue on the TF51 towards Vilaflor. Vineyards on walled slopes border the road as you rise up to **Vilaflor** (25km 🛉🍽⊕🏨M), the highest town on the island (1161m/3810ft). Nestled on the edge of a plain, this mountain settlement looks up onto the steep forested inclines that run down off the high mountain spurs above. Vilaflor is a good base from which to explore the Paisaje Lunar (Walk 7b).

From Vilaflor follow the TF21 north, passing some of Tenerife's loveliest Canarian pine forests. **Pino Gordo**, a *mirador* 2km past Vilaflor, sits amidst these regal ancient pines (🏨). Leaving the viewpoint, at Lomo Blanco you pass the track called 'Pista Madre del Agua' — another approach to the Paisaje Lunar (Walk 7a). Then the road climbs through spectacular mountain landscapes, passing **Las Lajas** *zona recreativa* 36km 🍴).

You enter **Las Cañadas**★ at the pass of **Boca Tauce** (42km 🅿), where Walk 6 begins and ends. The twisted uprising of rock over to the left here is more impressive when approached from this direction. A spell-binding lunar landscape unfolds before you. The constant change of colour and rock formation within the encircling crater walls is the highlight of this tour and, I imagine, of your visit. Sharp-surfaced lava flows give way to smooth mounds of scoria, while sunken gravel beds create 'pools' along the floor. Majestic El Teide is with you wherever you go, always more impressive from a distance.

Heading right at the pass, you first skirt the immense gravel plain called **Llano de Ucanca**, almost immediately passing its eponymous *mirador* (🏨). Further along, intriguing bright patches of blue and green rock in the roadside embankment catch your attention — **Los Azulejos** (The Tiles). Stop a while at the **Parador de las Cañadas** (49km 🏔✕𝒊), where Walks 7c and 7d begin, to admire the **Piedras Amarillas** (Yellow Stones; 🅿) and the **Roques de García** on the opposite side of the road. These strange rocky upthrusts, the most famous of which is shown overleaf, stand guard over the eastern edge of the Ucanca Plain.

Pass by the turn-off to the Teide funicular (you would waste most of the day queueing here) and continue via the **Tabonal** and **Minas de San José** viewpoints (🏨) to the **Cañadas Visitors' Centre** (𝒊wc). This is an excellent source of information on the national park, with a small museum and an hourly film show. While the park covers more than 720 sq km, its focal point is a huge crater with a diameter of almost 16km (10mi). In spring you may see the exquisite, 2m/7ft-tall *taginaste rojo* flowering here — a magnificent sight when its tapering stem is embellished with bright red florets. Immediately beyond the visitors' centre is **El Portillo** (64km ✕☊wc), the 'Little Gateway'.

From here head left, descending through pines. Soon there are views over the verdant north to Puerto de la Cruz and the built-up coastline. Keep an eye out for the **Mirador Piedra la Rosa★** (74km ☊), a viewpoint over a rock formation resembling a rose. You'll pass several roadside picnic areas (☊) before you come to the signposted turn-off to **La Caldera★** (81km ✕△☊ ☐wc). From this little crater (*caldera*), there are wonderful views over the green slopes of La Orotava and the sea.

Just below the La Caldera turn-off lies the **Aguamansa trout farm★** (82km ➤wc and ❀). From there lovely countryside

Roque Cinchado, the most dramatic of the Roques de García, has been incorrectly (but understandably) known as 'God's Finger' for years.

scenery of tilled plots amongst sagging, lichen-covered walls and scatterings of aged chestnut trees takes you down to **La Orotava★** (95km ✚☐⊕M), known for its Corpus Christi festival (May/June), when the streets are 'painted' with flower petals and coloured sand. Continue on the TF21 down to Puerto. If you're interested in botany (especially island flora), you might stop at the **Botanical Garden** (❀). The compact garden is well laid out and contains a substantial collection of tropical and subtropical plants. It's on your route, some 2km south of Puerto, in the suburb of La Paz.

Puerto de la Cruz★ (103km ✚☐⊕☐Mwc), once a small port serving the farming town of La Orotava, is a bubbly, rather pleasant resort — as resorts go. What little remains of the old town lies buried amidst hotels and apartment blocks. You may wish to visit the 17th-century remains of the old port's heritage: the church of Nuestra Señora de la Peña, the Chapel of San Telmo and the Castillo de San Felipe (now a restaurant). The Casa Iriarte, a charming 18th-century house, is held to be the best example of Canarian architecture in Puerto.

From Puerto take the motorway west towards San Juan de la Rambla, continuing on the TF5 for 'SAN JUAN DE LA RAMBLA/ ICOD' when it ends. The coastal road passes below cliffs towering up to the left, while breakers crash below on the right (113km ☐☐ **Mirador de San Pedro**; 116km ☊ **Barranco de Ruiz**). **San Juan de la Rambla** (119km ✕☐) is a charming, fresh-white village overlooking the sea. Las Aguas, a neighbouring village on the rocky shoreline below, is a

The famous dragon tree at Icod de los Vinos

picture-postcard scene glimpsed just before San Juan. All the way from Puerto to the northwestern tip of the island, you're immersed in banana palms and bright seasonal blooms.

Keep following the TF5 for 'ICOD' until you can fork right for 'ICOD' and 'GARACHICO' (TF42). Then stay on the TF42 until you can head right again, on the TF82 for the town centre. **Icod de los Vinos★** (129km ♞🏠⊕) is set on the fertile, vine-growing slopes below El Teide. No doubt you will want to see the famous ancient dragon tree and the nearby church of San Marcos (16/17C): to get there, go straight over the roundabout for 'DRAGO MILENARIO' (brown sign). Continue uphill and turn right just past the Shell station on your right. To avoid getting caught up in the narrow one-way streets by the church and tree, it's easiest to leave your car in the car park halfway up this street. Return the same way to the Shell station and head left to resume the tour.

Back at the roundabout, ignore the turn-off right to Playa de San Marcos, a resort that never took off with tourists, but is very popular with the locals — a small black-sand beach surrounded by dark jagged cliffs. Go straight over the roundabout, but then be sure not to turn right on the TF5; keep ahead for 'BUENA-VISTA' and 'GARACHICO' (TF42). Manorial homes amidst banana plantations come into view as you head west, soon hugging the coast. Come into **Garachico★** (135km ♞🍴🏠⊕M). This beautifully sited village, once an important port, was destroyed by a volcanic eruption in the early 18th century. But a few buildings of interest survive: the

16th-century San Miguel Castle, the Baroque palace of the Marqués de Adeje, the 17th-century Convent of San Francisco, and the Church of Santa Ana (founded in 1548). Garachico is also known for its inviting natural rock pools. The Roque de Garachico, rising off the shore, bears a cross to protect the site from another catastrophe.

Continuing west on the TF42 you pass through the narrow streets of **Los Silos** (141km ♞🏠🎋). Further along this coastal plain lies **Buenavista** (145km 🏠⊕🎋). The village is walled in by high sharp crags; gorges and valleys cut back into this cataclysm of rock. Just past the Plaza de San Sebastián and a small chapel on the right, turn left for 'PUNTA DE TENO'* — *if you're here Monday to Wednesday.* Some 5km along the TF445, there are especially fine views from the **Punta del Fraile** (📷), where the island falls away into an indigo sea. The road winds round and under rough indented

---

*The point is *closed to tourists' motor vehicles* from 10.00 to 17.00 Thu-Sun for reasons of conservation. You can still visit on foot, by taxi or on Titsa bus from Buenavista station (Tue-Sun every hour on the hour from 10.00-16.00, returning 25min later; fare 1€).

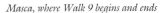

Masca, where Walk 9 begins and ends

cliffs, high above the sea, and then descends to the lighthouse on the dark volcanic promontory of **Punta de Teno** (155km 📷), one of the richest botanical areas in the Canaries. Swimming off the rocks in the crystal clear water here is a must!

Back at the junction in Buenavista (164km), turn right on the TF436 for 'EL PALMAR'. A steep climb through rocky terrain leads you up to El Palmar's lush valley, hidden far above the coastal plain. The reclining valley walls are terraced straight up to the crests. Go through **El Palmar** (170km) and, 1km further on, turn right on the narrow country lane for 'TENO ALTO', straight away passing **Los Pedregales** Visitors' Centre (*i*M⚲△ and Sunday morning farmers' market). Then continue the steep climb up this gorgeous road to **Teno Alto** (178km ✕📷) — a tiny outpost of farms scattered across a tableland. Try the home cooking in the restaurant here, especially the *cabrito* (kid) and *garbanzos* (chickpeas).

Then return to the El Palmar road and head right. At KM12 you come to the **Mirador de Baracán** (190km 📷) and can take in the dramatic difference

between the El Palmar and Masca valleys — the former smooth and sweeping, the latter sharp and turbulent. Then wind downhill into deep gorges on an increasingly vertiginous road, where various *miradors* (📷 and ✕ at **Cruz de Hilda**) open up magnificent views — especially over **Masca** (195km 📷 *P*), a favourite village amongst the islanders themselves. Walk 9 descends the spectacular ravine here (photograph page 62), a narrow corridor of 700m-high rock walls that ends at an equally spectacular beach.

Climbing out of the gorges, you quickly pass the starting point for Walk 8 (*P*) and cross another pass, where the **Mirador de Cherfe** (📷) opens far-reaching views to La Gomera, La Palma and El Hierro. Then begin the descent, with El Teide making a splendid backdrop. In the attractive village of **Santiago del Teide** (201km ✝⚲⊕🎋) turn right in front of the church on the TF42 for 'LOS GIGANTES'. In **Tamaimo** (208km ⚲), a village sheltering below a high rocky protrusion, turn right on the TF454 ('LOS GIGANTES'). Neatly laid out unobtrusive greenhouses cover the landscape, as the route winds downhill. At a T-junction (213km), keep right (same signposting). **Los Gigantes** (215km 📷) is a modern tourist complex, set against a backdrop of sheer cliffs★ rising vertically out of the sea. From here I prefer to go back to the TF47 and quickly make for 'LAS AMERICAS', but you *could* follow the built-up coast to **San Juan** (225km ⚲), and take the TF47 from there. At the roundabout below Adeje (Walks 3 and 4), turn right on the TF1, back to **Playa de las Américas** (240km).

Car tour 2: THE CUMBRE AND THE SUN-BAKED SOUTH

Playa de las Américas • Guía de Isora • Las Cañadas • El Portillo • Güimar • Arico • Granadilla • Playa de las Américas

212km/131mi; 5-6 hours' driving;
Exit B from Playa de las Américas
(plan on reverse of touring map)
En route: 🍴 at Chio, Forestal
Park, Los Frailes; Picnics (**P**
symbol on the touring and
walking maps) Boca Tauce,
Piedras Amarillas; Walks: (1, 3,
4), 6, 7. (Other walks and

secluded picnic spots are described in *Landscapes of Tenerife*.)
Driving is generally good, except for
some 30km of bumpy narrow road
along the TF28. The cumbre
above Arafo is often shrouded in
low-lying mists. Note that there are
no petrol stations en route between
Guía de Isora and Arafo.

From the greenest to the driest, from the lowest to the
highest, this drive has it all. The higher inclines along
the southern flanks of the island, missed by most tourists,
are a dramatic contrast to the rich green slopes of the north.

Set off from Exit B in Playa de
las Américas, heading north, at
first along the motorway. Below
Adeje (Walks 3 and 4), take the
TF82 for 'GUIA DE ISORA'. The
road gradually ascends, cutting
through rocky ridges and
dipping into *barrancos*. There are
uninterrupted views along a
coastline robed in banana palms.
Guía de Isora (19km 🍴⊕) is a
small country town sitting high
on the bare rocky slopes. It's
worth wandering the narrow
streets here.
At the far end of **Chio** (23km
🍴), turn right and right again
for 'EL TEIDE' (TF38). Las
Estrellas restaurant (✕🖼),
6.5km along, is a fine viewing
point over the southwest coast.
Pines begin appearing, scattered
across the landscape, and smooth
volcanic cones remind you of the
most recent volcanic outbursts.
Set amidst this scenery is the
lovely **Chio** *zona recreativa* (🍴).
The pines subside, and dark lava
flows spill across the landscape as
you approach **Las Cañadas★**.
Narices del Teide (50km 🖼), a
mirador at the foot of prominent
Pico Viejo on your left, allows
you to pull over to enjoy this
intriguing sight.
Coming to a T-junction at the

pass of **Boca Tauce** (53km **P**;
Walk 6), continue on the TF21
along the crater floor, with the
towering wall of peaks rising
impressively alongside you. El
Teide dominates the landscape,
but Guajara, Tenerife's third
highest mountain, projects
noticeably out of the crater walls.
The drive from Boca Tauce is
described in Car tour 1: use the
notes on pages 11-12 as far as **El
Portillo** (75km).
At El Portillo turn off right on
the TF24 to climb the *cumbre*.
Anthill-sized cones grow out of
the inclines below the road.
Retama (a hardy yellow-
flowering broom), white-
blooming *margarita del Teide* (of
the daisy family), and mauve-
flowering *alhelí del Teide* creep
across the terrain. The tones in
the gravel slopes change from
maroon, purple and black to
grey, mauve and russet. Mirador
La Tarta offers a fine view to El
Teide; nearby **La Crucita**
(90km 🖼; photograph overleaf)
is the point where pilgrims once
crossed the TF24 on their way
from the north to Candelaria for
the celebration of the Assumption of the Virgin of Candelaria,
Tenerife's patron saint.
Pines reappear and the country-

15

side becomes rockier, rougher. You snatch far-reaching views along the way from a series of viewpoints. First, a 1km detour to the left leads to the *miradors* of **Chimague** and **Chipeque** (📷): the latter looks out over the pine-wooded northern slopes to El Teide. **Ortuño** (📷) follows, with similar views. Past the large **Forestal Park★** (⛩) adventure centre at the KM16 road marker you come to the **Mirador Montaña Grande** (110km 📷), looking out over the verdant hills of La Esperanza, all the way to Santa Cruz and up to the Anaga range.

From here retrace your route for 12km, then turn left on the TF523, to descend to the sun-bleached south via Arafo and Güimar. Pines give way to loose scatterings of chestnuts, which cover the lower slopes, passing a viewpoint called **Montaña Colorada** (📷) and the turn-off to the **Monte Los Frailes *area recreativa*** (⛩). The Güimar basin opens up ahead, revealing great ravines cutting back deep into the steep escarpment. High brown stone terraces step the slopes of this productive agricultural centre. Vineyards interspersed with vegetable patches cover the greater part of the land. Bypassing the centre of Arafo, go straight through **Güimar★** (145km ⛽⊕ and the 'Pirámides de Güimar' **M**). The one-way system takes you to the right of the church, over a roundabout and to a right turn in front of city hall. You meet the TF28 in front of a petrol station: turn right (*not signposted*), cross a bridge, then continue ahead for 'FASNIA'.

This bumpy old road winds in and out of shallow ravines before climbing out of the basin along the eastern escarpment, from where you have a superb view over the valley and towards the Anaga Peninsula. From here on, the monotone landscape is more harsh. Trees have vanished, save for the fine-branched Jerusalem thorn bordering the roadside. In April and November its blossoms cheer up this countryside. Rock walls terrace the slopes. **Fasnia** (162km ⛽⊕) is a pleasant country village set back off the road. Between here and Arico, there are few settlements, and the land looks almost abandoned.

Keeping straight on through **Arico** (176km ⛽⊕), you eventually come to **Granadilla** (183km ✝⛽⊕), where intense cultivation returns to the the countryside. This important agricultural centre occupies one of the most fertile valleys in the south and boasts the best oranges on the island. Leaving the town, keep down to the left and follow the TF64 ('AUTOPISTA SUR') to the motorway, then head right to **Playa de las Américas** (212km).

El Teide dominates the skyline at the pass of La Crucita.

Car tour 3: QUIET CORNERS OF THE NORTHEAST

Playa de las Américas • Tacoronte • Bajamar • Punta del Hidalgo • Cruz del Carmen • Las Carboneras • Taborno • Pico del Inglés • La Laguna • Playa de las Américas

Reckon on 271km/168mi; 5-6 hours' driving; Exit A from Playa de las Américas (plan on reverse of touring map)
En route: Walks and picnic spots along this tour are described in *Landscapes of Tenerife*, which explores the Anaga in detail.

*Some 90min of this drive are spent on the motorway, getting to and from the northeast. **It is very easy to get lost** between leaving the TF1 and Bajamar, and in La Laguna: use your smart phone or good maps and plans! Driving on the Anaga will be slow on the tortuous roads.*

This short excursion visits varied landscapes. You'll drive down to the coast and take a dip in sea-water pools (there are several choices); continue up to the summits of the Anaga and go for a stroll in the laurel forest; then perhaps finish off the day with something of historical and cultural interest, sauntering around the streets of La Laguna.

Take the motorway (Exit A) and head east. **Candelaria★** (61km ♦♨⊕) is a good place for a break now or on your return. The large square on the seafront near the modern basilica (1958) is quite impressive, with its statues representing the ten former Guanche chiefs of Tenerife. The church houses the new statue of Nuestra Señora de la Candelaria, the island's patron saint. (The

original, purportedly found in 1390 by Guanche herdsmen, was lost in a tidal wave in 1826.) Rejoin the motorway and be sure to turn off at Exit 6 for 'LA LAGUNA', which takes you onto the Autopista del Norte (TF2). On this motorway, follow signs for 'TF5/LA LAGUNA', *not* Santa Cruz. Having joined the TF5, go

past La Laguna, all the way to Exit 21 for 'EL SAUZAL' (96km). Off the TF5, turn right at the roundabout for 'EL SAUZAL' (TF172). At the next round-about take the first exit for 'TACORONTE' (TF152).
In **Tacoronte** (98km ♦♨⊕), turn left on the TF16 for 'TEJINA' immediately past the plaza (with the bright green and glass modernistic 'sculptures'). If you would like to visit Tacoronte's 17th-century church (its wooden statue of Christ is attributed with many miracles), turn left at a roundabout with a dragon tree 1km along this road. Otherwise, keep ahead all the way to **Tejina** (108km ✕♨), where a one-way system oper-ates. At an unsigned T-junction go *left*. At the large roundabout outside Tejina, go straight over on the TF13 for 'BAJAMAR'. Colourfully blooming bushes and creepers, together with large banana plantations, enliven the landscape along here. The village's tidal pools make the small-scale resort of **Bajamar★** (112km ♨⊕) a popular swim-

Roque de Taborno is often called the 'little Matterhorn'.

(TF143) brings you to **Batán**, superbly sited in stunning mountain scenery.

Return from Batán to the TF12 and keep left for **Cruz del Carmen★** (154km ✗✝🖼*i*), with a visitors' centre of special interest to walkers. Beyond this viewpoint you leave the dense forest for a brief time, as you drive down to two more beautifully sited villages: 1km past the turn-off to Pico del Inglés, go left. At a fork, keep left (TF145) for 'LAS CARBONERAS'. Valleys open up as you descend, and Punta del Hidalgo reveals itself for a moment. Roque de Taborno, a perfectly formed spike, is a prominent landmark sitting high atop the opposite ridge. At a further fork again keep left. **Las Carboneras★** (165km ✗) sits glued to a hill, encircled by cultivation. Now return to the fork passed earlier (TF138) and turn left. After descending a forested ridge, you come into **Taborno★** (170km 🖼), where small dwellings are dispersed along the crest of the ridge, rising high above two *barrancos*.

Return the same way to the main road and turn right. Then head left to **Pico del Inglés★** (179km 🖼). Perched on the spine of this range that divides the island north and south, the *mirador* offers views down into the hidden cultivation of the Afur valley, catches snippets of the coast, and looks out to the island's guardian, El Teide.

From Pico del Inglés make for **La Laguna★** (191km ✝🏠⊕M) on the TF12. There's much to enjoy in this charming university town before you weave your way back to the motorway and head west to **Playa de las Américas** (271km).

ming spot. A backdrop of severe rocky ridges and ravines overshadows the settlement, and an abundance of xerophytic plants cling to the dark abrupt inclines. Continue on the same road to **Punta del Hidalgo★** (115km △🖼🚍). It lies along a slight bay with a rocky beach, across from Bajamar. The road ends past the village at a roundabout, where high craggy crests fall away into the sea.

Return to the roundabout outside Tejina and follow 'LA LAGUNA'. Follow the same signposting through **Tegueste** (126km ✗🚍). **Las Canteras** (131km ✗🚍) straddles a crest. At the roundabout up in the village, take the first exit, turning half right onto the TF12 ('LAS MERCEDES') and heading up into the magnificent laurel forest. The **Mirador de Jardina** (🖼) on the right, 4km from Las Canteras, gives you captivating views of the lush green undulating hills outside La Laguna. Under 2km further on, fork left to 'BATANES', to make for the isolated village of Batán, hidden in a valley deep in the spine of the peninsula. Keep right all the way downhill. Some 8km of winding road

18

Car tour 4: BUCOLIC CHARMS OF THE RUGGED ANAGA

Playa de las Américas • Pico del Inglés • Roque Negro • El Bailadero • Chamorga • Taganana • Almáciga • Benijo • San Andrés • Igueste • Santa Cruz • Playa de las Américas

Reckon on 262km/162mi; about 6-7 hours' driving; Exit A from Playa de las Américas (plan on reverse of touring map)
En route: ⊓ at the El Bailadero tunnel. (Walks and secluded picnic spots are described in *Landscapes of Tenerife*, which explores the Anaga in detail.)

Around 1h of the drive is spent on motorways, getting to and from the Anaga. Driving is slow in the mountainous terrain, with fairly heavy tourist traffic. Note: there are no petrol stations between Las Canteras (outskirts of La Laguna) and San Andrés — 83km along the touring route.

This excursion takes us amidst the mountains of the Anaga Peninsula. Twisting along the backbone of this range, the road is one continuous *mirador*. Inland, lost in these rugged contours, lie tiny remote villages, clinging to rocky nodules and buried in *barrancos*. And along the coast, quiet and secluded little bays unravel.

Start out as in Tour 3 (page 17), but shortly after joining the TF5, leave it again at Exit 8A: follow signs for 'TEGUESTE' (TF13). At the roundabout turn right for 'ANAGA'. Keep following 'LAS MERCEDES', first on the TF13, then on the TF113. Once in **Las Mercedes** (80km 🚗), go straight over the roundabout for 'CRUZ DEL CARMEN'. You pass a modern church on your right and join the TF12, where you keep straight on in the same direction, soon immersing yourself in the coolness of the laurel forest (⊓).
Stop at the **Mirador Cruz del Carmen** (🚗♦✕𝒊); its Visitors' Centre is a good source of information about the Anaga's walking trails. Then, 1km further on, turn right for **Pico del Inglés★** (88km 🚗), another fabulous *mirador* with far-reaching views. Head back to the main road (TF12) and turn right, after 1km passing Casa Carlos, a very popular base for hikers. Solitary houses speckle the ridges segmenting the isolated Afur Valley. Some 3km along, turn left on the TF136 for

Roque Negro (96km 🚗), a small, well-concealed settlement overshadowed by an enormous black basalt rock. The village square serves as a good look-out point: Afur can be seen far below in the shadows of these high crests, and a wild beach, the Playa del Tamadite, lies beyond the village. (I recommend a 4km detour to Afur, if only to visit the friendly bar!)
The main tour returns from Roque Negro to the TF12 and heads left. Ravines clothed in subtle shades of green slip off the southern slopes (104km 🚗⊓). At the 107km-mark, turn off left for **El Bailadero★** (🚗✕), the viewpoint from where the photograph overleaf was taken. Just 05.km past the hideous green buildings here (how did they let it happen in a protected area?) you pass the charming Albergue de Anaga, blending perfectly into the landscape — a truly get-away-from-it-all place to stay. From here on the road is flanked by dense laurel forest. Just before the κM6 road marker, at the **Mirador de las Chamucadas** (113km 🚗), you'll have

Walkers' signposting on the Anaga Peninsula; see comments on page 34.

good views down over Igueste, a seaside village built across the mouth of a *barranco* (visited later in the tour).

Descending in S-bends into open rocky terrain, you pass a turn-off right (117km) to Las Bodegas, a hamlet sheltering in a narrow *barranco.* La Cumbrilla is the village perched high on the ridge under which the road passes. **Chamorga**, the most isolated village on Tenerife, lies at the end of the road, a couple of kilometres further on. A smattering of white dwellings, the hamlet snuggles into the sides of a *barranco,* shaded by palms and loquat trees.

From Chamorga return to the Taganana turn-off (left, just below El Bailadero). Some 2km further down, turn left again (⌂). After passing through a tunnel under the Bailadero *mirador*, you overlook a landscape of razor-sharp ridges cutting down to the sea. **Taganana★** (139km ♦⊕), a brilliant array of white houses, is spread across the tumbling lower crests of the valley. Palms and colourful gardens make this settlement extremely photogenic. Roque de las Animas (the Ghosts' Rock), towers straight above the road 1km beyond the village. **Roque de las Bodegas** (141km) with its roadside restaurant, is a busy tourist stop. Past **Almáciga**, **Benijo** (144km ▭), where the tar ends, is just a few cottages high above a beach. But Restaurante El Frontón, with good food and magnificent views, is a pleasant place to take a break.

Retracing your route through the tunnel, follow the TF12 down the Barranco de San Andrés to the south coast. At **San Andrés** (163km ♟), turn left for Igueste. The palms of Las Teresitas (Tenerife's only golden-sand beach) add a touch of the tropics, and the unofficial naturist beach of Las Gaviotas is glimpsed far below, at the foot of the cliffs. Picturesque **Igueste** (171km ✕) sits at the end of this cliff-hugging coastal road. From Igueste follow the coast road all the way to **Santa Cruz** (185km ♦♟⊕). Try to pass through the city before (or well after) the rush hour! Then take the motorway (♟) back to **Playa de las Américas** (262km).

The stepped valleys of Taganana, from the Mirador El Bailadero

Car tour 5: LA GOMERA'S SOUTHERN LANDSCAPES

Valle Gran Rey • Arure • Las Hayas • Chipude • Alajeró • Playa de Santiago • San Sebastián • El Cedro • Los Roques • Laguna Grande • Valle Gran Rey

Reckon on 142km/88mi, 5-6 hours' driving. Join the tour at San Sebastián (page 25) if you come from Tenerife by car ferry.

En route: ⊼ at the Ermita de las Nieves, El Cedro, Laguna Grande; Picnics (**P** symbol on the touring and walking maps) Barranco de Arure, Mirador Ermita del Santo, La Fortaleza, Calvario, Targa, Pastrana, Degollada de Peraza, Caseta de los Noruegos, Pajarito; Walks: 10-16, 18, 19, 21-36, 39, (17, 20)

A long drive, with several interesting stops en route; an early start is recommended. The roads are good, but the link road between the GM1 and GM2, which serves El Cedro and Los Roques, is sometimes closed due to rockfall. The narrow crazy-paved road to El Cedro may be unnerving for some motorists. Be alert for foraging goats and sheep on the roads. Petrol stations en route are few and far between; their opening hours on Sundays and holidays may be restricted.

Y ou will be astonished at what this island of 378 square miles has to offer! This tour introduces you to the south of La Gomera, which at first glance appears bare, barren and sun-baked. For most tourists, perhaps it is. But *you* will find valley floors laden with produce, grassy saucer-shaped basins, elegant palm groves and pockets of pines. The out-of-the-way beaches (stony in winter, sandy in summer) will entice you to return for a 'beach day'. Heading back to Valle Gran Rey, you enter another world — a salubrious forest, dark and damp and dripping with moss. Short walks, perhaps to picnic spots, lead you through this relic of the Tertiary Period, to fern-drenched slopes and cascading streams. You needn't be a walker to enjoy this rare gift of nature, but you may become one!

Leaving **Valle Gran Rey★**, a dramatic climb takes you up the sheer walls of the Gran Rey *barranco* — the island's most picturesque valley (**P**; Walks 10, 11, 18 and 29). You look out over a verdant tapestry of palm and banana groves, gardens, and a stream bed filled with cane. Several *miradors* allow you to pull over and enjoy different corners of the valley. But the one not to miss is the **Mirador El Palmarejo** (8.5km ☞✕), high in the escarpment at the northern end of the valley. Designed by the late César Manrique, the beauty of this

unobtrusive viewpoint lies in the simplicity of design and decor — as with all his creations in his native Lanzarote.

Rounding the sheer walls of the Barranco de Arure (an adjoining valley), you soon pass the Bar-Restaurant El Jape in **Arure**, a suggested starting point for Walks 12-14, as well as Alternative walk 11. Just around the bend you will come to your turn-off right for Las Hayas (10km). But if this is the only tour you will be taking on La Gomera, first *turn left* at this junction for some 200m, then turn left again on a signposted lane to the **Mirador Ermita del Santo** (☎❀⬥Ⓟ). Some 300m along the lane, just beyond the path to the *mirador,* you'll find a parking area. This very dramatic viewpoint, visited during Walks 12-14, overlooks the isolated Taguluche Valley and the village of Taguluche some 500m/1650ft below. Return to the Las Hayas fork and head left.

The main tour keeps right at the Las Hayas junction. The road passes above the enchanting **Embalse de Arure** (en route in Walk 15) and climbs to the plateau, where you meander across an undulating tableland that rises up into the centre of the island. The islands of La Palma (with the twin 'humps') and El Hierro can be seen in the distance. La Fortaleza (Walk 22), the prominent buttress of rock up ahead, soon steals your attention. Coming into palm trees, you enter **Las Hayas** (15.5km ✖). Vegetarians may like to eat at La Montaña, where Doña Efigenia has been serving up the same local meal for decades. She's become quite famous — the place is mostly visited by tourists. If you decide to combine lunch here with Walk 16 or nearby Walk 17, be prepared for slow service and bring a jacket — the restaurant is not heated. Walk 15 calls at Las Hayas, and Alternative walk 42-2 starts here.

Leaving the village, you come to a junction at the edge of the laurel forest. Turn right for **El Cercado** (20km; Walks 19, 21), the centre for ceramics. This charming village, characterised by its rustic stone cottages, sits around a cultivated basin cut up into small vegetable gardens. You look across a hillside heavily lined with stone walls on the

The aptly-named peak of El Sombrero

approach to **Chipude** (24.5km). Walk 19 (a fairly easy circuit and *highly recommended for all sure-footed visitors*) begins and ends here, as does tough Walk 22. The village is also the starting point for Walk 18 and finish of Walks 21 and 23. Just outside Chipude, you pass the turn-off for La Dama; Chipude's petrol station (⛽) is 0.3km down that road. La Fortaleza (Ⓟ) now dominates the landscape with its massive crown of rock. Pines merge into the surrounding cloak of heather. The **Mirador de Igualero** (29km ⬥☎) gives you a chance to pull over and admire La Fortaleza in all its grandeur. Erquito is the sprinkling of houses in the *barranco* floor far below.

A short way further on, turn right for Alajeró and begin a drawn-out descent to Playa de Santiago. The countryside is bare of trees and heavily smudged with rock. You peer down into sheer-sided ravines that appear without warning. Elevated tongues of land dip towards the sea, terminating abruptly in cliffs. Luminous green *tabaiba* enlivens the sombre hillsides. Four kilometres downhill you

pass the **Mirador del Drago** (📷), from where there is a fine view over the harsh countryside. To see the dragon tree for which the *mirador* is named involves a 20-minute descent down a steep cobbled trail into the valley below and another 35 minutes to climb back up! Unfortunately, you can't get too close either — it's been fenced off.

One kilometre past the *mirador* you come to the turn-off left for Imada. The main tour continues straight ahead here but, were you to take a detour to the village, you would have some truly magnificent views from this road. Unfortunately, there are no lay-bys, so if you do pull over, *please be on the alert for other traffic!* Imada is a popular hiking centre (Walks 27-29), while Walk 26 cuts across this access road en route to the Barranco de Guarimiar.

Palms, dotting the inclines, announce the scattered village of **Alajeró** (37.5km ♦). Take the first turning right, down to the church square. To get back to the main road, take the first left turn just below the church. But first, if you'd like to stretch your legs, you could take a short walk

(25min return) up to the **Ermita San Isidro** on **Calvario**: after turning left below the church, take the first right (with purple signpost for the *ermita*). Drive straight ahead all the way to the end of the tar at the foot of the peak (map on page 97). From there a paved path leads to the summit chapel (🅿) with its fine view towards La Fortaleza and Garajonay.

Beyond Alajeró you're soon looking across to Tenerife, made bold by the prominence of El Teide; this magnificent sight will remain with you all the way to San Sebastián. Two picturesque hamlets — Targa and then Antoncojo — huddled up against rocky outcrops on your left may catch your attention as you descend through this dusty, thirsty landscape. The turn-off for Targa (Walks 25 and 26; 🅿) is passed at 40km and later the island's tiny airport — the most beautiful in the Canaries, but with hardly any flights, since the ferry connections from Tenerife are so good.

Banana plantations sitting back off the sea-cliffs betray **Playa de Santiago★** (51km ⚓⊕) below, at the confluence of two large

ravines. As you approach down the most westerly of the ravines (Barranco de los Cocos), keep right for the port. This once-quiet fishing village has grown rapidly, with apartments and timeshares taking advantage of the best weather on the island, and little shops and restaurants strung out along the waterfront to cater for tourists. Turn left at the seafront, where Walks 25, 30, 32 Alternative and 33 end. Just before the road begins to climb out of the second *barranco* (Barranco de Santiago), you could take a 5km return detour up the east side of the *barranco:* take the next road off left, sign-posted to 'PASTRANA/TACO'. Non-walkers might especially enjoy this drive, to see the tucked-away hamlets of Taco, El Cabezo, El Rumbazo (Walks 26, 28) and Pastrana (Walks 28 and 30; *P*). These four settlements sit in the shadows of towering jagged walls, overlooking a valley floor crammed with gardens and orchards. This oasis of greenery is the last thing you would expect to see when you enter this initially inhospitable-looking gorge. Pastrana also houses a friendly little restaurant with outdoor terrace, serving local specialties in a beautiful setting (closed Mondays).

The main tour bypasses this turn-off and, on reaching the main road, heads right, zig-zagging up out of the Barranco de Santiago past banana groves, vineyards and avocado plots. This is the domain of Fred Olsen, the Norwegian shipping magnate, who developed the large Jardín Tecina Hotel, as well as the golf course and the Pueblo Don Tomas urbanisation above it. Steadily climbing, you enter a landscape carved up by more impressive ravines,

separated by razor-sharp ridges flecked with *tabaiba*. Pockets of palms occupy corners of the *barrancos*. Further inland, pines, splashed in amongst *Cistus* and prickly pear, add more hues to the greenery.

A short way past the KM1 road marker you pass parking for Walk 32, then quickly come to a junction at the **Degollada de Peraza** (65.5km ✗☞*P*). Stop at the *mirador* and look at the clean-cut Las Lajas Valley and its delightfully-stepped reservoirs. Circular walk 31 would take you high up this appealing gorge. There's also another short detour possible from this pass: you could follow the Hermigua road to the left for 1km and then take the first right turn you come to. This leads to the well equipped Ermita de las Nieves *zona recreativa* (🍴♨).

The main tour keeps *right* at the pass, to continue through a land-scape littered with stone walls. The ridges no longer burst up angrily out of the valleys. El Sombrero, a hat-shaped rock adorning a parallel ridge, steals your attention five minutes down. Then the verdure in the hillsides slowly fades, and the landscape becomes barren and sun-baked once more. You pass a turn-off to the villages in the Barranco de Las Lajas and then come into **San Sebastián** (82.5km ♨🚌⊕ M), where Walk 33 begins and Walk 34 ends. This is a charming little town with some lovely pedestrian areas and plenty of small bars where you can enjoy a drink or a coffee. For those in search of history, there's the Church of the Assumption, where Columbus supposedly attended mass before setting off on his historic journey to the New World; also Columbus's house (Casa de Colón) and the

The lovely setting of the Ermita de las Nieves area recreativa

simply-built Torre del Conde (Count's Tower, a 500-year-old fortress built by Felipe II). The last now houses a small museum with artefacts from La Gomera and South America, dating back to the period before the Spanish Conquest.

Leave the town on the GM1, rising north past the bus station. The wide valley floor narrows to a 'V'. Sharply outlined ridges run down off the *barranco* walls. Closer to the *cumbre*, the craggy slopes are greener. Just past the KM7 road marker, you pass two cottages on the right and the (unsigned) **Camino Forestal de Majona**, at a place called **Las Casetas**, where Walks 34 and 35 begin and Walk 36 ends. Then pass an equally unheralded viewpoint on the left, just before a tunnel (**Mirador de los Manaderos**, shown on pages 112-13). From this northbound road you have an even better view over the reservoirs in the Barranco de las Lajas. In winter the valley comes to life, when the streams are full, and water cascades over the reservoir walls. The road curls up the *barranco,* in and out of tunnels. Scarred cliffs tower above.

Leaving the south, you pass the Bar Cumbre restaurant (✕) and soon duck into a long tunnel.

Emerging on the north side of the island, a completely different landscape awaits you: heather and strands of laurel forest cap the summits and trail down the upper inclines. Sheer dome-shaped peaks stand shoulder-to-shoulder over on the right. A parking place (🅿) just outside the tunnel exit enables you to pull over and enjoy this sudden change of scene. You get a taste of the north — of Car tour 6. Views encompass the banana plantations of Hermigua below.

A little over 1km further on, *at a rather dangerous blind corner* (97km), turn left for 'EL CEDRO' and head up into the **Garajonay National Park★**. This amazing, well-engineered road snakes up the precipitous wooded slopes of the *cumbre*. Springs trickle down out of the mossy banks. House-leeks of different shapes and sizes speckle the rock faces and white-to-carmine-coloured flowers *(Senecio)* fleck the shady banks. Lichen-clad heather and moss-covered laurels shade the route. The air is damp; for much of the year, the *cumbre* lies shrouded in mist, which has a special beauty all its own. The *miradors* of **El Rejo** (🅿) and **El Bailadero** (🅿) will more than likely be in cloud.

Chejelipes, in the Barranco de Las Lajas — a possible detour off the GM1 just outside San Sebastián

growing straight up out of the sweeping Barranco de Benchijigua. El Teide rises in the background, beyond the finely-etched ravines of La Villa and Las Lajas. Another balcony, on the left-hand side of the road, looks out onto the stouter rocks of Ojila, Zarcita and Carmona (from left to right). A fourth *mirador* lies just below these two.

Return to Cruce de la Zarcita and turn left. Shortly after you remount the *cumbre*, be sure to pull over at the **Mirador de Tajaqué** (📷) and take in the panorama over the immense Barranco de Benchijigua on the south side of the ridge (Walk 30). Just 100m short of the KM22 road marker, you pass a track junction at the left of the road near the aerial-topped **Caseta de los Noruegos** (🅿; see the caption with the photograph on page 28). At the **Pajarito roundabout** (116km; 🅿), where Alternative walk 26 begins, keep right towards Laguna Grande. You could climb to Garajonay's summit from here (Walk 27), but an easier ascent begins 1km further on, at **Alto del Contadero** (Short walk 23).

Pass the **Laguna Grande** picnic area (120km ✕⛱) and, at the next junction (**Cruce de las Hayas**) head left. Then take the first right, back to to **Las Hayas**. From here follow your outgoing route to return to **Valle Gran Rey** (142km). Descending into this grand valley at sunset, you find the *barranco* in another mood: its austere façade is softer, and the walls no longer frown down upon you. If you haven't fallen in love with La Gomera by now, you never will.

Soon (103km), at a place called **Reventón Oscuro**, you come to the turn-off for 'EL CEDRO'. Don't miss this scenic hamlet! Midway down the crazy-paved road there is a fork: a motorable track off left (signed 'ARROYO DE EL CEDRO') leads into the centre of the forest (to the Las Mimbreras parking area and circular Walk 24); a right takes you down to **El Cedro★** (✕⛱), where the only parking is at the picnic area or the Restaurante La Vista. You really need half a day to explore the hamlet and the enchanting forest with its picnic area on foot: see Walks 23, 24 and 39.

Returning from El Cedro, you mount the crest of the *cumbre* and soon reach a junction, the **Cruce de la Zarcita** (111km), where Walk 23 begins. Turn left here. After 0.5km you come to one of the island's most famous viewpoints — **Los Roques★** (📷). It's an intriguing place, where four enormous pillars of lava (the remains of volcanic chimneys) burst up out of the landscape. The two viewing platforms on the right overlook Roque de Agando (where Walk 30 starts) — a massive protrusion

Car tour 6: LA GOMERA'S VERDANT NORTH

Valle Gran Rey • Las Hayas • Laguna Grande • Hermigua • Agulo • Garajonay National Park Visitors' Centre • Vallehermoso • Arure • Valle Gran Rey

102km/63mi; 4-5 hours' driving. If you come from Tenerife by car ferry, join (and leave) the tour at the Garajonay junction: head north up the GM1 and pick up the notes at the 36km-point (page 28).
En route: ⩎ at Chorros de Epina, Laguna Grande, (Jardín de las Creces and Raso de la Bruma are not far away); Picnics (Ⓟ symbol on the touring and walking maps) Garajonay, Caseta de los Noruegos, Agulo, Presa de Meriga, Mirador Rosa de las Piedras, La Meseta, Mirador

Ermita del Santo; Walks 10-16, 18, 20, 23, 26, 29, 30, 36-43, (17, 44)
Roads are winding, with some rough patches: driving will be slow. The link road between the GM1 and GM2, which serves El Cedro and Los Roques, is sometimes closed due to landslips/rockfalls. Watch out for foraging goats and sheep on the roads. Only three petrol stations en route: at Valle Gran Rey, Hermigua and Vallehermoso; on Sundays and holidays their opening times may be restricted.

The perfect way to begin this drive is to catch a sunrise from atop Garajonay. The majestic beauty of El Teide, in rapidly changing hues of gold, orange and mauve, afloat on a sea of white clouds, is a sight you'll long remember. But if you're not an early bird, the sunset is often equally rewarding. On this tour you delve into the rugged north, where narrow ravines carve up the countryside. Hillsides, patched in scrub and capped with woods, are discernably greener than in the south. Banana palms, orchards and garden plots fill the stream beds, intensifying the greenery. Tall palms gracefully ornament picturesque villages. But alas, all too frequently a cape of cloud descends before midday — another good reason for an early start.

Follow Car tour 5 as far as the junction just beyond **Las Hayas** (16.5km). Here keep straight on (the left fork) and, when you come to a T-junction (**Cruce de las Hayas**), turn right. Crossing the rolling hills of the island's centre, you thread your way through heather and laurel. Pine woods appear in the background. You pass the sunken *zona recreativa* **Laguna Grande** (21.5km ✕⩎). The restaurant here, with its cosy fireplace, is worth keeping in mind if you hit one of the cold spells that the island sometimes saves up for visitors. A meal here will set you up for any drop in temperature!

If it's a fine day, you'll want to climb **Garajonay★** for the extensive views. The easiest route is from **Alto del Contadero**, 2.7km beyond Laguna Grande. Pull into the large parking area on your left and climb the signposted track opposite, using the notes on page 86 (Short walk 23). It takes about 20 minutes to reach the summit. On the ascent, you look across pine trees to the imposing rock, La Fortaleza. As the name suggests, it resembles a fortress. On clear days, the view from Garajonay (Ⓟ) encompasses El Hierro, La Palma, Tenerife and Gran Canaria.

27

From the signposted track junction 100m past the KM22 road marker, a track leads to fine views over the Barranco de Benchijigua and to Roque de Agando and even La Fortaleza in the distance. But the devastating forest fires of 2012 began here, and it will be some years before this picnic spot is at its best again.

Continuing the tour towards Hermigua, enjoy more superb views off either side of the *cumbre,* the island's backbone. Keep left at the **Pajarito round-about** (25km), where Alternative walk 26 begins. Some 0.7km further on, 100m past the KM22 marker stone, you pass a sign-posted junction on the right. A gently descending track turns off right here, near the aerial-topped **Caseta de los Noruegos** (Ⓟ; see photograph caption above). Twisting down through the laurel forest, you come to **Cruce de la Zarcita** (29km), starting point for Walk 23. Turn left here to make for the north. (But if you're not doing Tour 5, first continue to the right, to see **Los Roques★** (Walk 30), described on page 26.)

Plump peaks, all in a line, rise abruptly up out of the valley over to your right. On route to Hermigua you pass the forestry road to El Cedro (see Car tour 5, page 26), followed by the two *miradors* of **El Bailadero** (☜ on the right) and **El Rejo** (☜ on the left). At the junction where you join the GM1 (36km), turn

left. Some 2.7km along, you may wish to take a road off left to the landmark Roques de San Pedro — two pointed upthrusts often referred to as the 'Twins'. It's a detour of about 1km. From there you could follow Walk 39 for 20-30 minutes, to explore the Barranco del Cedro — the lushest gorge on the island (see page 121).

Hermigua★ (44km ✝♨⊕M) is a striking contrast of white houses and green banana groves. Hamlets step corners of the ravine walls and stretch along the floor. Fruit trees grow amidst the houses. Walks 37-39 start and end here, while Walk 36 begins here. Three places you might like to visit are the Los Telares Museum (a small collec-tion of traditional household utensils), the old Dominican convent a short way further along the road, and the Ethno-graphic Museum another 650m downhill.

As you leave Hermigua, a 4km return detour to the right, signed 'EL PESCANTE', would take you to the old port, where there's a natural rock pool dramatically set at the foot of a sheer escarpment — a tremendous setting. (*Note:* The best and safest swimming on the island is on the south coast. The north is often rough and can be extremely dangerous: even the pool here is safe *only* when the sea is *dead calm!*)

Leaving this valley, you see Tenerife sitting across the water straight in front of you. A *mirador* (👁) allows you to pull over safely to admire it. Then, climbing high above the sea, you round a bend and look over what has to be the most beautifully situated village on the island. **Agulo★** (47km 🛉👁) is set in an alcove of rocky cliffs, high above the sea, looking straight out towards El Teide (🅿). Wander along the cobbled alleys that pass through the banana groves and admire the archetypal houses that give this village so much character. Walk 40 starts here; Walk 41 starts and ends here.

A tunnel leads you out of Agulo's natural amphitheatre of cliffs into a deep, sheer-faced ravine. Rock walls rise above you. Reaching the upper confines of this *barranco*, you come to **Las Rosas** (52km), a scattered farming village. Fork left on a road signposted for 'LA PALMITA' and the national park. Walkers and nature enthusiasts alike will find a wealth of information at the **Juego de Bolas★**, the **Garajonay National Park Visitors' Centre** (*i*), 3km uphill. There's a typical Canarian dwelling, a display of local handicrafts and a film about the national park. Walks 40 and 41 — both strenuous hikes — pass this way. But Short walk 41 to the awesome **Mirador de Abrante★** (👁✗) above Agulo is only half the huff and puff — just 55

minutes return (see pages 128 and 129).

Another short ramble most easily reached from here is Walk 44, which visits a reservoir, the **Presa de Meriga** (🅿). Allow about 8.5km return for this detour. To get there from the Visitors' Centre, head south on the Laguna Grande road for 2.7km, then turn left at an inconspicuous wooden sign for 'PALMITA'. After 1.4km *ignore* the sharp left turn to Mériga; keep ahead to a sign, 'PRESA DE MERIGA'. This is a great excursion on a foggy day, when the dead tree trunks rising straight up out of the tiny reservoir give the walk a fairy tale flavour. But when we last checked just before press date, the reservoir was closed for works — so it may be enlarged in future.

Return to the junction in Las Rosas and turn left. After 0.3km you could take another 6.5km return detour to an out-of-the-way viewpoint and picnic spot — but this one is only worth the effort on fine days. Turn sharp left up the steep lane signposted 'PRESA AMALAHUIGUE' and climb straight up past the square in Las Rosas to the **Amalahuigue Reservoir**. Cross the dam wall and then turn left, remaining on the same road all the way up. You climb a scruffy, shallow ravine as far as the tree line at **Rosa de las Piedras**. Visit the **Mirador Rosa de las Piedras** (👁✗🅿) on the crest of the ridge. From here, a vast cauldron stretches across in front of you, and ridges pour down into it. The restaurant Roque Blanco (closed Mondays) here serves up hearty local food in a friendly atmosphere.

The main tour, however, continues towards Vallehermoso. You look down into plunging ravines that drop off into the sea. Terraced vineyards ladder the slopes. These slopes produce the best wine on the island. Swinging inland, you wind around large open valleys, passing above the pretty village of Tamagarda, noted for its typical oblong houses, all with tiled rooftops. Tamagarda's restaurant makes a mean *tortilla de ajo* (garlic omelette). Palms adorn the hillsides, and Roque El Cano, the massive lava pillar shown on page 127, bursts upon the scene: sitting like an exclamation mark, it punctuates the end of a trailing ridge.

Another tunnel takes you into the cauldron, and you're engulfed by hills. Roque El Cano looms overhead. The farming settlement of **Vallehermoso** (69km ♣☎⊕) soon unfolds, tucked up against the valley walls. Dust-brown slopes climb back off it. A stream of banana plots, fruit trees and gardens flows down the valley floor, reviving the landscape. Walks 42 and 43 begin and end here. Apart from the walks, whenever I reminisce about this village my thoughts turn to *miel de palma* — palm honey. It's made by boiling the palm sap and leaving it to cool into a dark syrup. Try this mouth-watering recipe: mix *gofio* (roasted maize flour; see the footnote on page 98) and the honey (as much as you like) into a doughy mixture, add pieces of white cheese (*queso blanco*), lemon rind, and ground almonds … and life will never be the same again! Sample the good local wine and the *mistela,* a local liqueur.

Turn right at the roundabout in the centre of Vallehermoso and right again at the T-junction that follows ('PARQUE MARITIMO'). *Please note* that the beach at

Playa de Vallehermoso (71km) is extremely dangerous at *all* times, hence the swimming pool nearby, which is only filled in summer. The setting, however, is wonderful. The 'castle' over to the left (Castillo del Mar) was once a banana-loading station. Some years ago it was developed as a cultural centre and restaurant, but closed due to financial problems.

From the beach, return to the junction, and keep right to circle above Vallehermoso. Climbing out of the valley, its bucolic charm becomes more evident. You look out over adjoining valleys laced with palms. Plots of potatoes and tomatoes sit squeezed along the *barranco* floors and into the gentler pauses in the walls. The striking hamlet of Macayo captures your attention, its simple stone dwellings clinging to the side of a palm-studded ridge on your left. You can look down on this enchanting scene from the *miradors* a few bends higher up the road.

Approaching the summits, the countryside is scruffier, with scrub running down the declining ridges. In spring the route is splashed with resplendent yellow-flowering *codeso*. Near the tree-line you pass the **Camino Forestal de la Meseta** signposted 'PRESA DE LOS GALLOS' (82km ℗; Walk 42) and then the turn-off for Alojera and Taguluche (83km). These isolated villages rest amongst dry, denuded hills, completely cut off by the cloud-catching *cumbre*. This scene will have much more impact from the Mirador Ermita del Santo later in the tour.

In the meantime, just around the bend, you come to the restaurant Chorros de Epina (✗). Alternative walk 42-1 is based here, but it's quite a long trek. So try something shorter: from the parking area follow the sign 'CHORROS DE EPINA' down a crazy-paved path; then, *before* the chapel, go right down the GR to the seven springs, the **Chorros de Epina** (⛩). On your return, follow the path *behind* the chapel (⛪🏞) for a few minutes. In spring you'll stumble onto a habitat of the precious pink-flowering Canary geranium, and shortly thereafter you will be looking through the trees onto Epina, an exquisite little hamlet resting at the foot of the escarpment amidst green garden plots.

Leaving Chorros de Epina, keep zigzagging uphill in the company of El Teide. Your vista sweeps back across the gently-declining coastal hills and over the numerous gullies segmenting the great cauldron. Heath trees, growing out of cracks in the rock, lean out over the road, and you disappear into the forest. At the Arure/Laguna Grande junc-

tion (the first you encounter), keep right. (A left turn here would lead to two more picnic sites in a wonderful stretch of forest — Raso de la Bruma and Jardín de las Creces — Walks 17 and 16 respectively.) Approximately one kilometre further on you pass the *mirador* of **Alojera** (🏞).

Leaving the forest, descend to **Arure** (91km; Walks 12-14), the home of a delicious honey. Some quaint stone cottages rest alongside the garden plots lining the floor of the *barranco*. At the end of the village (0.2km before the Valle Gran Rey junction), branch off right to the **Mirador Ermita del Santo** (🏞⛪🅿), unless you stopped there earlier in the day. This superb viewpoint hangs out from the escarpment high above Taguluche, a remote pocket of civilisation sitting deep in a bare landscape ruptured by upheavals of sharply eroded hills. Heading home, follow your outgoing route back to **Valle Gran Rey** (102km).

A river of trees on the road to Taguluche (Walks 13 and 14); do make time to visit this village and take in the views from the chapel shown on pages 70-71.

⚘ Walking

This book includes 16 long and short walks reached quite easily from a base in the **south of Tenerife**, but I've emphasised walking on **La Gomera**. (The companion volume, *Landscapes of Tenerife,* describes 65 long and short walks in the north and east of Tenerife.)

There are walks in this book for everyone.

Beginners: Start on the walks graded ● or ● — or walk to a picnic spot (see page 8); most of the picnic suggestions make good short and easy walks.

Motorists: I have increased the number of circular walks in this edition; almost every walk can be done from a car — and I've given you waypoints for the parking place so that you can set your satnav/GPS. But some walks are unavoidably linear: a good solution is to walk from A to B and take a bus back to your car — or, where timetables permit, drive to the end of the walk, leave your car there, and take a bus back to the start.

Experienced walkers: If you are used to rough terrain and have a head for heights, you should be able to tackle all the walks in this book —

taking into account, of course, the season and weather conditions. For example, in rainy weather some of the walks will be unsuitable — especially the Barranco de Masca on Tenerife (Walk 9) and any walk on La Gomera involving narrow paths with steep ascents and descents. Always read the 'Grade' section of every walk you plan to do!

All walkers: Be sure to check for any updates on Sunflower website *before* you walk! See the *'UPDATE'* tab on the Gomera page.

The sandstone funnels of the Paisaje Lunar (Walk 6)

Grading, signposting/waymarking, maps, GPS

We've tried to give you a quick overview of each walk's **grade** in the Contents. But some walks have shorter or alternative versions, and in the Contents we've only had space to show the *lowest* grade of a *main* walk: for full details — including easier versions — see the walk itself. Here is a brief overview of the four gradings:

● very easy — more or less level (perhaps with a short climb to a viewpoint); good surfaces underfoot; easily followed

● easy-moderate — ascents/descents of no more than about 300-500m/ 1000-1800ft; good surfaces underfoot; easily followed

● moderate-strenuous — ascents/descents may be over 500m/1800ft; variable surfaces underfoot — you must be sure-footed and agile; possible route-finding problems in poor visibility

● expert — only suitable for very experienced hillwalkers with a head for heights; hazards may include crossing landslides or edging along very narrow paths with no respite from constant exposure

Any of the above grades may be followed by:

⦙ *possibility* of vertigo — for those with no head for heights at all
⦙⦙ *danger* of vertigo — you must have a very good head for heights

Signposting and **waymarking** on both islands has been upgraded to European standards. There are two types of walks:

■ long-distance footpaths ('Grandes Recorridos' or 'GR' routes), indicated by *red and white* waymarks;

■ day trails which, on Tenerife, may be prefaced by 'PR' (for 'Pequeños Recorridos') and indicated by *yellow and white* waymarks or 'SL' (for 'Senderos Locales') and indicated by *green and white* waymarks. On La Gomera these routes are usually just numbered and marked *green and white* (although you may see some older yellow/white waymarks).

For all routes, horizontal stripes (=) indicate 'continue this way', angled (∠) or right-angled stripes show a change of direction; an 'X' (✕) means 'wrong way'.

Most signposting on **Tenerife** conforms to European guidelines, as can be seen in the photo on page 20, where PR trails are signposted yellow/white. But *in addition* the Teide National Park has maintained its own longstanding system of route marking for 35 walks within the park. These are usually indicated on green metal signs showing route numbers. The map on page 56 shows three over-lapping types of route: the long-distance GR 131, two different day (PR) walks and several national park trails.

Gomera adopted the European guidelines in 2004, but due to cost constraints has since abandoned numbering and colour-coding of PR and SL routes, although GR trails are still marked red/white. Instead there are currently 40 signposted and green/white waymarked government-maintained trails (see photograph on page 119), *plus* 18 marked trails in the Garajonay National Park. All official trails are shown on a map, *Camina La Gomera,* published by the island government and available at the Juego de Bolas Visitors' Centre, where you can also get a brochure about the national park trails.

The **maps** in this book are based on Openstreetmap mapping (see page 2), but have been very heavily anno-tated from notes and GPS work in the field. It is a pity that we have to reproduce them at only 1:50,000 to keep the book to a manageable size; quite a few walkers buy both the paperback *and* download our pdf files so that they can print the maps at a larger size — or you can enlarge them on a photocopier.

Two things to note about the maps: firstly, *both* islands have official trails *and* national park trails, and sometimes the numbers overlap — confusing! So on our walking maps official island trails and GR routes are identified in purple type, while the national park trail numbers are printed in green. Secondly, the walks in this book ***do not always follow the 'official' routes***, so please read the walking notes!

Free **GPS track** downloads and **height profiles** are available for all the walks: see the Gomera/Southern

Tenerife page on the Sunflower website. Please bear in mind, however, that GPS readings should *never* be relied upon as your sole reference point, as conditions can change overnight. *But even if you don't use GPS,* the maps are now so accurate that you can easily compare them with the maps on your smartphone and pinpoint your exact position. And it's great fun is dragging the GPX files over Google Earth to preview the walks in advance!

Dogs — and other nuisances

There are few nuisances to worry the walker on either Tenerife or La Gomera. The **dogs** tend to *look* more vicious than they really are — especially the shepherds' dogs. But your biggest concern is likely to be abandoned dogs trying to follow you back to wherever you are staying. Nevertheless, you may wish to invest in a 'Dog Dazer' — an ultrasonic device which persuades aggressive dogs to back off without harming them. These are available from various websites, including Amazon.

Hunters blasting their shotguns will scare the wits out of you. During the autumn hunting season you may prefer not to hike on Thursdays, Sundays or public holidays. Usually you hear hunters long before you see them.

You'll be happy to know that there are *no* poisonous snakes or insects on either island.

Weather

Island weather is often unpredictable, but there are a few signs and weather patterns that may help you forecast a walking day. Tenerife and La Gomera are blessed with good walking weather all year round.

The north unfortunately has more than its fair share of rain, but boasts pleasant temperatures. The south soaks up the sun. Las Américas/Los Cristianos on Tenerife and Playa de Santiago on La Gomera enjoy the best weather. On La Gomera, Valle Gran Rey is slightly cooler and is prone to strong winds. Wind also strikes the southern coastline east of Los Cristianos, but rain is rare. During the winter months, the north not only suffers from clouds, but often experiences very strong winds, especially on the more open hilltops. Walking and keeping upright at the same time can be a problem!

Apart from the seasons, the **weather patterns** are influenced by two main **winds**: the *alisio*, the trade wind from the northeast, and the *calima,* an easterly or south-easterly wind. The trade wind is identified by the low-flying fluffy clouds which hover over the north (between 600-1500m/2000-5000ft) for much of the year. On Tenerife, you can head to Las Cañadas to get above the clouds and enjoy clear blue skies. But on La Gomera, the *cumbre* (central mountain chain) and Garajonay usually remain deep in cloud — not much fun for walking, since it's cold and wet, with zero visibility. The walks in the north of La Gomera all disappear into cloud at some stage. Sometimes, however, the summits sit just above the sea of clouds — a wonderful sight.

The *calima,* quite different, brings heat and dust from the Sahara. Temperatures rise considerably, and the atmosphere is filled with very fine dust particles. This weather is more frequent in winter than in summer. It seldom lasts more than three or four days. These days, outside of summer, are good for walking; even if it's a little warm, the sky is cloudless, although hazy. (In summer it is *not* advisable to walk when the *calima* is blowing; you risk sunstroke and dehydration, unless you are in a very shaded area.)

Two less frequent winds that could spoil your day are the nor'westerly from the North Atlantic and the sou'westerly from the tropics. Both bring heavy rains. This weather covers the entire island and can last a few days. When these winds blow in winter, Las Cañadas and El Teide are more likely to see snow than rain.

Remember (especially in winter) that no matter how wonderfully the day begins, it could deteriorate. **Always be prepared for the worst.** Along Gomera's *cumbre* the weather is less predictable still, and it can be ***exceedingly cold***. Remember too, that the sun can be your enemy, perhaps especially on days of light cloud cover.

Where to stay

If you are based in the La Caleta–Los Cristianos axis in the **south of Tenerife**, the entire island is within reach if you have a hired car. A few superb walks are also nearby (Walks 1-9 in this book). The bus service is also excellent — you could even explore the Anaga Peninsula via Santa Cruz using the companion volume, *Landscapes of Tenerife*. Another advantage of staying at the *playas* is the proximity of the ferries — ideal for day trips to nearby La Gomera.

But if the sight of concrete jungles 'turns you off', try El Medano, Adeje or Granadilla. For something really special, you could stay in a **rural hotel or house**: see www.

ecoturismocanarias.com. Consider, too, spending a night at the Parador de las Cañadas to enjoy the night sky! Then you could start Walk 7 there, approaching the Paisaje Lunar from above. To book, log on to www.parador.es/en/parador-de-las-canadas-del-teide.

Exploring **La Gomera** from a base in southern Tenerife is the way many visitors will first become acquainted with this little-developed gem of an island. The car tours and some short walks are perfectly feasible on day trips.

But to get to know La Gomera on foot, you will want to be based on the island. Most visitors stay at Valle Gran Rey or Playa de Santiago, followed by San Sebastián and, to a lesser extent, Hermigua and Agulo. San Sebastián's Parador (www.parador.es/en/parador-de-la-gomera) is set above the town, with great views. (Like the rest of the hotel, its excellent restaurant is themed around the era of Columbus, who set sail from San Sebastián on his first voyage across the Atlantic.) But there is also a good selection of self-catering accommodation, *pensions,* and rooms to rent all round the island. See the website for rural hotels and houses mentioned above, or surf the web.

Camping is forbidden anywhere inside the national parks or designated protected areas.

What to take

If you haven't packed any special equipment — like a rucksack or walking boots — you can still do some of the walks, or buy some equipment at one of the sports shops. Don't attempt the more difficult walks without the proper gear. For each walk in the book, the *minimum* equipment is listed. Where walking boots are required, there is, unfortunately, no substitute: you will need to rely on the grip and ankle support they provide, as well as their waterproof qualities. All other walks should be made with stout lace-up shoes with thick rubber soles, to grip on wet or slippery surfaces, unless I specify that trainers are adequate.

You may find the following packing list useful:

walking boots	up-to-date bus timetable
mobile/smartphone/gps	small rucksack
waterproof rain gear (outside summer months)	plastic bottle with water-purifying tablets
long-sleeved shirt (sun protection)	long trousers, tight at the ankles
first-aid kit, including bandages	insect repellent
walking stick(s)	knives and openers
windproof (zip opening)	lightweight fleece, warm fleece
map (see page 34)	extra pair of socks
spare bootlaces	plastic groundsheet
sunhat, sunglasses, suncream	torch, whistle, compass

Please bear in mind that I've not done *every* walk in this book under *all* weather conditions. Use good judgement to modify my lists according to the season.

Country code for walkers and motorists

The experienced rambler is used to following a 'country code' on his walks, but the tourist out for a lark may unwittingly cause damage, harm animals, and even endanger his own life. A code for behaviour is especially important on Tenerife and La Gomera, where the rugged terrain (and unexpected cold weather at high altitude) can lead to dangerous mistakes.

- **Only light fires** at picnic areas with fireplaces.
- **Do not frighten animals**. The goats and sheep you may encounter on your walks are not tame. By making loud noises or trying to touch or photograph them, you may cause them to run in fear and be hurt.
- **Walk quietly** through all hamlets and villages and take care not to provoke the dogs.
- **Leave all gates just as you found them**, whether they are at farms or on the mountainside. Although you may not see any animals, the gates *do* have a purpose: they keep animals in (or out of) an area. Again, animals could be endangered by careless behaviour.
- **Protect all wild and cultivated plants**. Don't try to pick wild flowers or uproot saplings. They will die before you even get back to your hotel. Obviously fruit and other crops are someone's private property and should not be touched. *Never cross cultivated land.*
- **Take all your litter away with you.**
- **DO NOT TAKE RISKS!** This is the most important point of all. Some of the walks cross remote country and can be both *very cold and potentially hazardous.* Distances on both islands are deceptive — perhaps with exhausting descents into and ascents out of hidden *barrancos* between you and your goal. Only link up walks by following routes indicated on the walking maps; don't attempt to cross unmapped terrain. *Never walk alone,* and *always* tell a responsible person *exactly* where you are going and what time you plan to return. Remember, if you become lost or injure yourself, it may be a long time before you are found. *Always be prepared for bad weather,* and on any but a very short walk near villages, be sure to take a first-aid kit, mobile, torch, whistle, compass, extra water and warm clothing — as well as some high-energy food, like chocolate.

Spanish for walkers

In the tourist centres most people speak English. But once out in the countryside, a few words of Spanish will be helpful, especially if you lose your way. Here's a way to communicate in Spanish that is (almost) foolproof. First, memorise the few short key questions and their possible answers below. Then, when you have your 'mini-speech' memorised, always ask the many questions you can concoct from it **in such a way that you get a 'sí' (yes) or 'no' answer.** Never ask an open-ended question such as 'Where is the main road?' Instead, ask the question and then *suggest the most likely answer yourself.* For instance: 'Good day, sir. Please — where is the path to Épina? *Is it straight ahead?*' Now, unless you get a '*sí*' response,

Margarita de piedra — the famous 'stone daisy' on the Las Cañadas road (Car tour 1)

try: '*Is it to the left?*' If you go through the list of answers to your own question, you will eventually get a '*sí*' response — probably with a vigorous nod of the head — and this is more reassuring than relying solely on sign language.

Following are the two most likely situations in which you may have to practice some Spanish. The dots (...) show where you will fill in the name of your destination. Approximate pronunciation of place names is in the Index.

■ Asking the way

The key questions

English	Spanish	pronounced as
Good day, sir (madam, miss).	Buenos días señor (señora, señorita).	**Boo**-eh-nos **dee**-ahs sen-**yor** (sen-**yor**-ah sen-yor-**ee**-tah).
Please —	Por favor —	**Poor** fah-**voor**
where is	dónde está	**dohn**-day es-**tah**
the road to ... ?	la carretera a ...?	la cah-reh-**teh**-rah ah ...?
the footpath to ...?	la senda de ...?	lah **sen**-dah day ...?
the way to ...?	el camino a ...?	el cah-**mee**-noh ah ...?
the bus stop?	la parada?	lah par-**rah**-dah?
Many thanks.	Muchas gracias.	**Moo**-chas **gra**-thee-as.

Possible answers

English	Spanish	pronounced as
is it here?	está aquí?	es-**tah** ah-**kee**?
straight ahead?	todo recto?	**toh**-doh **rec**-toh?
behind?	detrás?	day-**tras**?
to the right?	a la derecha?	ah lah day-**reh**-chah?
to the left?	a la izquierda?	ah lah eeth-kee-**er**-dah?
above/below?	arriba/abajo?	ah-**ree**-bah/ah-**bah**-hoh?

■ Asking a taxi driver to return for you

English	Spanish	pronounced as
Please	Por favor	**Poor** fah-**voor**
take us to ...	llévanos a ...	**Yay**-vah-nos ah ...
and return	y volver	ee vol-**vair**
for us at ...	para nosotros a ...	**pah**-rah nos-**oh**-tros ah ...

Point out the time when you wish him to return on your watch.

Walkers' checklist

The following points cannot be stressed too often:

- **At any time a walk may become unsafe** due to storm damage or road works. If the route is not as described in this book, and your way ahead is not secure, do not attempt to go on.

Canary bellflower
(Campanula
canariensis)

- **Walks graded for experts** may be unsuitable for winter, and all mountain walks may be hazardous then.
- **Never walk alone.** Four is the best walking group: if someone is injured, two can go for help, and there will be no need for panic in an emergency.

Cerrajón
(Sonchus ortunoi)

- **Do not overestimate your energies** — your speed will be determined by the slowest walker in your group.
- **Transport connections** at the end of a walk are vital.
- **Proper shoes or boots** are a necessity.
- **Mists** can suddenly appear on the higher elevations.

Palo sangre (Son-
chus tectifolius);
below: *Taginaste
rojo* (Echium
wildpretii)

- **Warm clothing** is needed in the mountains; even in summer take some along, in case you are delayed.
- **Extra rations** must be taken on long walks.
  Mobile, compass, whistle, torch, first-aid kit weigh little, but might save your life.
- **Always take a sunhat with you**, and in summer a cover-up for your arms and legs as well.
- **A stout stick/walking pole** is a help on rough terrain and to discourage the rare unfriendly dog.

Organisation of the walks

The walks in this book are located in the south and southwest of Tenerife and all over La Gomera. On La Gomera, the walks are arranged anti-clockwise around the island, starting from Valle Gran Rey (VGR). Bus journey times *from the nearest base* are indicated, both for outward and inbound travel. For motorists, GPS coordinates are given for the best parking places.

You might begin by considering the large touring maps inside the back cover. Here you can see at a glance the overall terrain, main and secondary roads, and the locations of all the walks. Flipping through the book, you'll see that there is at least one photograph for every walk.

Having selected one or two potential excursions from the map and the photographs, turn to the relevant walk. At the top of the page you will find planning information: distance/time, grade, equipment, and how to get there. If the grade and equipment specifications are beyond your scope, don't despair! You might be able to reverse the walk (go *downhill*) or else just do *part* of the route, turning back wherever you like. Look at page 8 as well; you can use the maps for short walks to some pleasant picnic spots.

When you are on your walk, you will find that the text begins with an introduction to the overall landscape and then quickly turns to a detailed description of the route itself. **Times** are given for reaching certain points in the walk. *Important: do* compare your own times with those in the book on one or two short walks, before you set off on a long hike. Remember that I've included only *minimal stops* at viewpoints; allow ample extra time for photography, picnicking, or swimming. If you are not a reasonably fit walker, these walks may take you *twice as long! Do* take this into account, especially when using public transport ... or when it's late in the day. I recommend that you start with a few of the shorter walks so you'll have some idea of how your pace compares with mine.

Below is a key to the symbols on the walking maps:

═══	motorway	●►	spring, tank, etc	♟/✝	church; shrine
═══	main road	Ⓟ	picnic spot (page 8)	⊡	cemetery
═══	secondary roads	PR TF 7	official island trail	帋	picnic tables
──	motor/jeep track	8	national park trail	并人	pylon; mast
─ ─ ─	trail, path or steps	☞	best views	▥	map continuation
6 →	main walk	🚌	bus stop	i	visitor centre
12 →	alternative walk	🚗	car parking	☼ ∩	mill; cave
12 →	other described walk	⚓	ferry port	Δ	rock formation
4/GR 131	official (signed) trail	■	specific building	I I	dyke; gate
── 400 ──	altitude (metres)	═══	park boundary	⦂	danger! vertigo!
		───	watercourse, pipe	❷	waypoint

Walk 1: MONTAÑA GUAZA

See photograph page 14
Distance: 11km/6.8mi;
3h25min
Grade: ● moderate, with a stiff
climb to the summit (428m/
1403ft) and a sometimes skiddy
descent; careful footwork needed
on the clifftop path. *No shade.*
Equipment: walking boots,
walking pole(s), sunhat,
suncream, light fleece, raingear,
picnic, plenty of water
Access: 🚌 (Timetables 2-4, 7-
10) to/from Los Cristianos;
alight at the bus station. Or 🚢
(Timetable 18) to the port. Or
🚗: park in the southeastern part
of town near the Costamar

apartments (28° 2.670'N,
16° 42.609'W).
*Short walk: Los Cristianos —
plateau — Los Cristianos*
(8km/5mi; 1h50min). ● Moderate ascent of 200m/656ft, *but no
shade.* Equipment, access as
above. Follow the main walk to
the 40min-point (❷), turn right
on the track and carry on from
the 2h10min-point to the end.
Alternative suggestion (13km/
8mi; 4h). ● The clifftop path
you leave to ascend Guaza runs
to the LIGHTHOUSE at Punta
Rasca and Las Galletas; it's
fairly easy, but sometimes
skiddy: you must be sure-footed.

Montaña Guaza is the oversized hill to the east of Los
Cristianos. While it doesn't inspire you to put on
your hiking boots straight away, it *does* make a most
rewarding evening's hike, especially around sunset.

The walk starts from the southeastern end of the seafront
promenade (◐) near the tall
COSTAMAR apartment building.
Follow the wide track off the
promenade, through a parking
area and behind the stony
naturist beach. Five minutes
along, take the hillside path by
the sign *'MONUMENTO NATURAL
MONTAÑA GUAZA'*. The path
bends hard right where another
path comes in from the left (❶):
make sure you turn left here on
the main, well-worn path; it will
take you along a dry, dusty and
stony hillside all the way to the
top of the plateau. Prickly pear,
candelabra spurge and *tabaiba*
are the few inhabitants of this
barren landscape. Ignore all
descending paths.
Reaching the PLATEAU, keep left
along its edge, skirting above a
valley. You briefly head alongside a WATERCOURSE (30min),
before veering off right to cross
abandoned terracing. Just after
encountering the watercourse

again, you come to the end of a
track. Turn left here, still on a
path, beside the valley.
You then meet another track
(❷; 40min), where you turn
left. *(But the Short walk descends
this track to the right.)* As the
ascent begins, fine views unravel.
Montaña Rasca is the volcanic
cone on the sea plain due south;
the lighthouse of the same name
stands behind it. Las Galletas is
the first of the settlements (see
Alternative suggestion above).
Further up the hill you're overlooking a couple of pastoral outposts. In the winter, goatherds
roam these hills.
Forty minutes up the track, the
way forks (1h20min). Keep
right for the summit, a good five
minutes uphill. The SUMMIT OF
Montaña Guaza (❸; 428m/
1403ft; 1h25min) is decorated
with various antennas. Your
views stretch up the backbone of
the island to the rim of Las
Cañadas. Sharp pinnacles and
ridges rise out of the barren

landscape, while bright white villages sprawl across the lower slopes.

From here a rough track takes you down to another *SUMMIT* (❹; 405m) with more aerials … and a bird's-eye view over Los Cristianos and Playa de las Américas further west. A couple of minutes more downhill, a two-minute detour to the right leads another viewpoint, directly above Los Cristianos.

Circling the mountaintop, you rejoin your *ASCENT TRACK* (1h55min) and follow it downhill to the right. Ten minutes down, when you reach the bend in the track that lies above the pastoral outposts seen earlier, pause to trace out your onward route back to the coast. Looking a little further down the track, you'll see derelict buildings on either side of the track. Not far past these ruins, a clear path — your ongoing route — can be seen etched across the plateau immediately below, running towards the sea.

Five minutes later you pass the point where you joined the track on your ascent (❷; 2h10min). Continue straight ahead here for another seven minutes (or about four minutes below the derelict buildings), to where the main track swings 90° left and a lesser track goes right. Keep straight

ahead here (❺), on a faint track, crossing another track forking off to the right. The track you are on quickly fades out, but your continuation, a faint path, can be seen up ahead — about 20° off to the right.

Less than ten minutes across the rock-strewn plain, a path joins from the left (2h35min): follow it to the right. Within the next five minutes, pass a turn-off left and come to a T-junction. Turn left here. At the next T-junction go right. A large *CONE OF GRAVEL* stands slightly to the left now — it's a good look-out point but, if you continue straight on past the cone to the clifftops, there's a good view over Palm-Mar, a small tourist village to the left.

Now returning to town, keep left from the clifftop viewpoint. In a couple of minutes a steep, slippery descent takes you across a shallow *barranco*. Gaining the crest, Los Cristianos and Las Américas reappear. These resorts are seen at their best from the edge of the cliffs (3h), especially when the paragliders add their flourishes of colour to the landscape. Follow the path along the clifftops until you rejoin your outward route. Turn left, back down to the beach. Five minutes later you're back at the *COSTA-MAR* building (❶; 3h25min).

Walk 2: ROQUE DEL CONDE

Distance: 5.2km/3.2mi; 3h30min (by 🚌 add 2km/ 25min overall)
Grade: ● a fairly strenuous ascent/descent of about 500m/

1650ft. The final 100m/330ft of ascent to the summit is steep, stony and slippery *(care needed on the descent!)*. Green/white waymarked SL TF 218.

Equipment: walking boots, walking pole(s), sunhat, suncream, warm fleece, windproof, raingear, picnic, water
Access: 🚗: park in Vento (signposted west off the TF51 in Arona), to the right of the Christ statue (28° 6.105'N, 16° 41.222'W). Or 🚌 to/from Arona (Timetables 4 and 6); journey time from Los Cristianos 20min. From the bus stop continue straight ahead across the bridge over the TF51. Then turn right immediately and head down to the road. Follow the TF51 uphill for a few minutes, then turn left into Vento. In five minutes reach a Christ statue at a junction, where the walk starts.

The table-topped summit of Roque del Conde is the most prominent feature of the landscape in the south of Tenerife. Unlike Guaza (Walk 1), it *does* inspire you to put on the hiking boots — it's obviously a mountain that is there to be climbed. Its eye-catching shape also makes one feel that it was probably once a sacred mountain.

Start the walk at the junction with the **CHRIST STATUE** (◯) in **Vento**. Conde stands bold as brass straight before you here. Head left at the junction (the best parking is to the right of this junction). Under 100m to the left, in front of house No 78, turn right on a lane. Then continue down the path that leads off it (WALKERS' SIGNBOARD for the green/white waymarked SL TF 218 and red/white waymarked GR 131). Passing between terraced gardens, after less than 50m the path swings back right, dropping into the **Barranco de las Arenas**. Out of the *barranco* you cross a crest, then dip into a side-stream full of rushes (**Barranco del Ancón**). In summer the countryside is as dry as a bone. The only plant life appears to be *tabaiba*, rock-roses and prickly pear.

Some 50m further along, the GR 131 heads off to the right (❶). Then, just after stepping over a narrow WATER CHANNEL (**15min**), you descend a well-paved trail into the deep **Barranco del Rey** (❷). Fig trees growing out of the valley walls supply the only greenery here. (Before climbing out of this *barranco*, head along to the left for a look at the high dry cascade.)
Out of the *barranco*, continue to the left. Paths head in all directions here, so follow the clear, green/white waymarked path — basically keeping left, beside the edge of the *barranco*. Rounding the hillside, you come to an ABANDONED BUILDING and plots (❸; **35min**). From here you have a good view back down over Arona.
Your continuing trail lies behind

44

View north to the hills from Playa de Adeje: from left to right, Roque de los Brezos, Roque Imoque, and table-topped Roque del Conde

the building. Minutes up, you pass above two THRESHING FLOORS — the second (**④**) is the larger and most impressive. The hillside above is stepped with a mass of stone-walled terraces. Approaching the top of the crest, the previously well-manicured trail becomes a rough path. Large clumps of candelabra spurge and prickly pear abound, the latter covered in pale yellow blooms in late summer.

Mounting the **Centinela ridge** south of Conde (**⑤**; **1h**), you look down on the blinding-white swathe of the *playas* — Los Cristianos and Las Américas. Your immediate surroundings are severe and colourless. The path, unclear initially, continues to the right, around the slopes of Conde; keep an eye on the GREEN DOTS AND CAIRNS. Several minutes along, a DYKE cuts across in front of you (**⑥**). Head along to the left; a steep winding ascent follows.

Some 20-25 minutes above the dyke, you're on the PLATEAU (**⑦**) below Conde. The first thing you'll notice is the remains of

extensive terracing covering this tableland, testifying to intensive cultivation in the past. Now it's just about five minutes more to the TRIG POINT at the SUMMIT OF **Conde** (**⑧**; 1001m/3283ft; **1h50min**).

If you've beaten the clouds, you'll have a 360° view across the surrounding farm settlements, the coastal plain below, and the pine-speckled backbone of the island. To the south of the summit, you'll find another THRESHING CIRCLE, and to the left of that, a MEMORIAL PLAQUE.

For the return, remember that the initial part of your descent is very steep and slippery! Allow 1h30min to retrace your steps to **Vento** (**O**; **3h20min**). Bus users: when you reach the TF51, cross it and head into the back of the village. Keep right past the magnificent square, full of Indian laurel trees, to make for the BUS STOP at the end of the street. (Halfway along you'll pass the restaurant El Patio, where they serve up good, reasonably-priced cooking in a cool courtyard.)

Walk 3: BARRANCO DEL INFIERNO

Important note: Because of its fragile ecosystem, this *barranco* is now within a Protected Natural Area; access is limited to 300 people per day. *You must book in advance to do this walk, choose your time slot for setting off, and arrive 15 minutes in advance.* The walk is open 08.00-18.00 daily *except public holidays,* and there is an entrance fee of 8 euros for adults (half price for children). You can book in person, by telephone (922 780 078) or online at www.barrancodelinfierno.es.
Distance: 8km/5mi; 2h40min
Grade: ● moderate climb/ descent of 300m/1000ft requiring some agility. The *barranco* may be impassable after heavy rain or rockfall, in which case it will be closed.

Equipment: walking boots, sunhat, fleece, windproof, picnic, water
Access: 🚗 to Adeje. If you're early enough, you can park near the start of the walk at the top of Calle Los Molinos (28° 7.575'N, 16° 43.427'W). To get there, turn left by the church at the top end of Calle Grande and follow the brown sign for the *barranco* (see violet line on the map). Otherwise there is a car park at the foot of Calle Los Molinos. Or 🚌 to/from Adeje (Timetables 5, 9); journey time from Los Cristianos 30min. Alight at the 'Cerco' bus stop and walk uphill through Plaza Venezuela to the roundabout, then up Calle Grande to the church; follow the same route as motorists (above).

The Barranco del Infierno (Hell's Ravine) has been the most walked gorge in the Canaries, with the resulting damage to flora and fauna. Visitor numbers are now strictly limited, as stated above. It is expensive, but with only 80 people allowed in at any time, the walk is more pleasant than in the crowded past. This *barranco* boasts one of the few permanent streams on Tenerife. High sheer walls close in on you, as you make your way up the defile of jagged rock. Wild blackberry drapes itself over the trees and bushes, and ivy 'tunnels' convey you up to the splendid falls. Adeje, set at the foot of the ragged crags that confine Hell's deep chasm, is an immaculate village, with an appealing combination of old and new.

The walk begins from the top of CALLE LOS MOLINOS (○) in the upper, older part of **Adeje**. Take the path between the *mirador* and the Restaurante Otelo, descending to the right, into the *barranco*. From the outset you're looking down into a dry ravine: further up the *barranco*, the water has been diverted for irrigation in watercourses and pipes. Clumps of prickly pear, *balo* bushes and *tabaiba* coat the steep slopes, and white daisies grow alongside the

path. The route is well marked throughout; please keep to the designated path.
On rising to a *mirador*, **Acequía Larga** (❶; **15min** — add 15 minutes to all times if you came by bus), you enjoy a fine view down the *barranco* and over Adeje, built at the very edge of the *barranco* walls. Fifteen minutes later there is another fine VIEWPOINT (❷). Soon after, you descend to the FLOOR OF THE RAVINE.
From here on the walk requires a

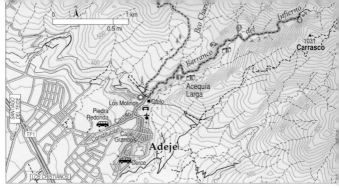

bit more agility, but this is the most beautiful and most dramatic part of the hike. When you come upon the STREAM (❸; **45min**), the bed of the *barranco* comes alive with willows and a tangle of bramble, shrubs and ferns. Pools become frequent and, if you're early, you will see and hear many birds.

The rocky path criss-crosses the stream between the perpendicular walls of the gorge. Close to the end of the passable section of the ravine, a soft mossy rock face, dripping with water, is seen. It's a slithery couple of minutes' walk to the right to see the lovely three-tiered WATER-FALL (❹; **1h20min**) splashing down some 80m/250ft into a small pool. The *barranco* walls tower 1000m/3300ft above you here, virtually blocking out the sky.

Allow another 1h20min to return to *CALLE DE LOS MOLINOS* for your car (❍; **2h40min**) — or 10 minutes more for the BUS STOP in **Adeje** (**2h50min**).

The newly rebuilt path in the barranco *is beautifully engineered.*

Walk 4: FROM LA ESCALONA TO ADEJE

Distance: 13.8km/8.6mi; 4h30min

Grade: ● moderate, with an ascent of some 200m/250ft and descent of 900m/2950ft (much of the latter on an skiddy trail demanding full concentration; walking poles are an advantage). All on waymarked trails (PR TF 71.2, then PR TF 71)

Equipment: walking boots, walking pole(s), sunhat, warm fleece, windproof, picnic, water

Access: 🚐 to the 'Ifonche' bus stop on the outskirts of La Escalona (Timetables 4, 7); journey time from Los Cristianos 30min. Return on 🚐 from Adeje (Timetables 5, 9); journey time to Los Cristianos 30min

Short walk: Barranco de la Fuente from Ifonche (5.5km/ 3.4mi; 1h30min). ● Fairly easy, with an overall ascent of 100m/ 330ft. Equipment as above. Access by 🚗: From the TF51 to

Vilaflor, turn left on the TF567 for Ifonche. At a crossroads by the friendly Restaurante EL DORNAJO (closed Thursdays), go straight ahead; then park 100m uphill, near the INFO BOARD for the PR TF 71 and GR 131 (❶; 28° 8.121'N, 16° 41.447'W). Follow the main walk from the 1h-point to the 1h45min-point (❺). You can turn back here, but it's worth carrying on and rising up the far side of the *barranco* for 10-15 minutes — to where a spectacular view greets you as you look back the way you came. Return the same way.

Alternative walk: Hardy hikers who don't like road-walking but don't mind climbing, see the map for Walk 5 overleaf: you could follow the well signposted and waymarked GR 131 from Arona to Ifonche or could take the 'El Topo' trail to El Refugio and continue from there (allow an extra 500m/1640; 1h30min).

M uch of this walk takes place in the cool and shady protected pine wood sliding off the island's backbone 1000m above sea level. Views trail you all the way up the modest ascent from La Escalona. But the best views on the walk are at the Boca del Paso: enjoy them while you can, because the descent from this pass will demand your full concentration!

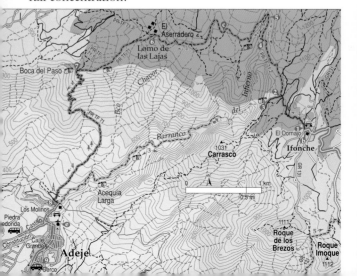

Starting from the 'IFONCHE' BUS STOP on the TF51 (○), follow the road uphill past a pretty CHAPEL (ⓐ) with a poignant statue of 'Hermano Pedro' and his dog in front and Roque Imoque in the background. You then pass a track off left to the restaurant El Refugio (Walk 5). Arriving at the restaurant EL DORNAJO in **Ifonche** (ⓑ; 1h), walk straight over the crossroads for 100m, then take an eroded track on the right (❶; PR TF 71/ GR 131 INFO BOARD). Just 50m along the track, at a FINGERPOST for the yellow/white-waymarked PR TF 71.2 to ADEJE, turn left on a trail that initially follows the line of a concrete WATER CHANNEL down to the left.

Keep to the well-waymarked path which quickly enters a light pine wood. Soon you can see an isolated farmhouse ahead. The path heads in that direction, passing an amphitheatre of old terracing on the left. Closer to the farm you cross a motorable track and then another almost immediately. This latter track is signed left to 'LA VISTA' (❷): follow it past the farmhouse to an old THRESHING FLOOR on the ridge (❸; 1h15min), from where there is a wonderful view deep into the **Barranco del Infierno** some 250m/800ft below.

(From the threshing floor this track continues as the 'Camino Carrasco' to Adeje — a possible variation for experts; it is not an officially way-marked or maintained route —

sometimes on skiddy stones and vertiginous in places.)

From the threshing floor return to the PR TF 71.2 and continue to the left. The trail rises gently through light pines to the crest of the ridge, where it becomes a lovely high-level walk above the deeply etched 'Hell's Ravine' below to the left. Under 20 minutes from the 'La Vista' signpost, the PR keeps right uphill at a fork (❹); the fork to the left goes to a spring and the floor of the *barranco*. Not far ahead the PR also drops to cross the stream bed (here called the **Barranco de la Fuente**; ❺; 1h45min). Grand specimens of Canarian pine grow out of the valley wall.

The path then rises up the western flanks of the *barranco* — a stiff climb lasting a good 10 minutes. Once at the top of the ridge, head along to the right. And it's not over yet: there are quite a few ups and downs ahead as the way now winds in and out of small *barrancos*. Notice the absence of under-growth here, typical of Canarian pine forests.

A little over 15 minutes from crossing the Barranco de la Fuente you come to a fork (ⓒ). The main, PR-waymarked trail heads right here (although you *could* go left along the flank; the paths rejoin). The PR rises to a SIGNPOSTED CROSSROADS in a clearing on the next ridge (**Lomo de las Lajas**; ❻; 2h30min). Here you *leave* the PR TF 71.2, which goes ahead to La Quinta; keep left on the PR TF 71 for ADEJE.

Crossing bedrock, the trail runs parallel with an IRRIGATION CHANNEL cut into the rock face. You pass below the few stone houses of **El Aserradero**, a small derelict hamlet where the saw-

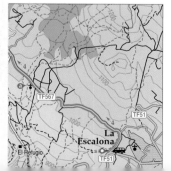

At the start of the PR trail you come into a light pine wood — refreshing and sweet-smelling — a nice picnic spot.

Margarita (Argyranthemum)

Balo (Plocama pendula)

Sea fennel (Crithmum latifolium)

Red-flowering tabaiba (Euphorbia atropurpurea)

Vinagrera (Rumex lunaria)

mill was once important to the local economy (*aserradero = sawmill*).

After 20 minutes a rocky promontory is reached at the **Boca del Paso** (**7**; **3h**). From this pass there is a wide view down over the tourist developments splashed along the southwest coastline coast between Los Cristianos and Los Gigantes. And looking up at the central massif, El Teide can be seen peering over the rim of the crater. Across the *barranco* to the right lie the farming villages of La Quinta and Taucho. The signposted TF 71.1 heads right from here to those villages, but you now keep left downhill, still on the signposted PR TF 71 for ADEJE.

The inclines are covered in the hardy omnipresent *balo, tabaiba,* and prickly pear. Not that you may notice: this is the start of a stony, skiddy trail that demands your full concentration as it descends in tight serpentines. After an uncomfortable 45 minutes you come upon the remains of TERRACING, with a

few tired almond trees. Half an hour later, below a RADIO MAST, I suspect you'll be grateful to have asphalt underfoot when you meet a road. Follow this road (**8**; CALLE DE LOS MOLINOS) past the starting point for Walk 3 and then steeply downhill. Take the first or second left turn to the CHURCH (**C**) in **Adeje**. Turn right in front of the church and follow the main street, CALLE GRANDE, to PLAZA VENEZUELA. At the bottom of the plaza is the 'CERCO' BUS STOP (**9**; **4h 30min**)

Walk 5: THE SUAREZ-TOPO CIRCUIT

Distance: 6.3km/4mi; 2h15min
Grade: ● moderate, with an ascent/descent of about 360m/1180ft. All on green/white SL-waymarked trails (not numbered at press date) or the red/white waymarked GR 131
Equipment: walking boots, walking pole(s), sunhat, warm fleece, windproof, picnic, water
Access: 🚗 to the old 'La Granja' restaurant on the TF51 a little over 1km north of Arona. Park north of the building, by a walkers' signboard set back off the road (28° 6.464'N, 16° 41.161'W). If the limited parking space is full, there's more parking round the next northerly bend. Or 🚐

to the 'Las Casas' bus stop about 1km north of Arona (Timetables 4, 7); journey time from Los Cristianos 30min. From the bus stop walk north to La Granja.
Alternative walk: _Suárez-Topo and Ifonche_ (9km/5.6mi; 3h).
● moderate; ascent 500m/1640ft. Equipment, access as above. Follow the main walk to the second threshing floor (**7**) and the lane below, then turn left for an easy high-level walk past a _PARAGLIDING LAUNCH_ (**a**) to _EL DORNAJO_ (**b**) in **Ifonche**. Turn right on the road (TF567) for 1km, then turn right on the track to El Refugio (**8**) and pick up the walk again at **9**.

This walk combines two of Arona's _senderos locales_ to make a very popular circuit. The individual paths, Suárez and Topo, both connected Ifonche with Arona and were used by the inhabitants for transporting lumber, livestock, crops and the like. The old farm buildings add even more interest to a walk rich in far-reaching views, both inland and to the coast.

Starting out at the _WALKERS' SIGNBOARD_ (**O**), take the track ahead, quickly crossing the **Barranco del Ancón** and coming to a fork (**1**) in front of a small _RESERVOIR_. Go straight ahead (right) here on the _GREEN/WHITE-SIGNPOSTED CAMINO SUAREZ_. (The north-bound Topo trail will be your return route.) At the next fork, where the main route appears to turn right alongside the lip of the _barranco_, keep straight on. You pass the _CASA DE ANCON_ (**2**); its old bread oven is pictured on the information board for the walk).
Then the trail dips to the floor of the **Barranco del Rey** (**3**): keep right here for about 20-30m, then the path rises out of the stream bed to the next ridge. In only three minutes the _RED/WHITE WAYMARKED_

GR 131 joins from the left (**4**). Follow it to the right, past old abandoned terraces and up to the **Degollada de los Frailitos**

Roque Imoque rises behind the beautiful threshing floor at the 1h20min point in the walk. Paragliders are often seen here; the Alternative walk passes their launching place.

(fairly easy) or **Roque Imoque** (hair-raising) in about 20 minutes.

From this threshing floor follow the sign 'FUENTE DE LAS PILAS' through an eroded area, over to an abandoned house. The green-marked trail then descends into the **Barranco del Rey** once more (where a five-minute detour would take you to a signposted SPRING). On the far side of the wide stony river bed, rise up past terracing to a MOTOR TRACK (**8**) and follow it to the right, to the charming restaurant EL REFUGIO (**9**; **1h35min**; open Oct-Apr, closed Sat).

From the restaurant the track deteriorates rapidly to an eroded ridge path (the CAMINO DEL TOPO) running parallel to a water pipe and IRRIGATION CHANNEL. After some 20 minutes a ruined farm lies below your path; 20 minutes later you return to the sign-posted fork (**1**) and then the starting point (**0**; **2h15min**).

(**5**; **30min**). From this saddle — where Roque del Conde (Walk 2) seems within arm's reach — there's a fine view down over the southwest coast.

The GR continues to the right, over the ridge, through pock-marked karst-like terrain. After a good 20 minutes you reach a saddle with a first THRESHING FLOOR and lovingly-built (but abandoned) terracing. This idyllic landscape surrounds the grand old CASA DE SUAREZ (**6**; **50min**), for which the trail is named. Take a break here, and let it all wash over you. Just half an hour later you come to another saddle, with another large, beautiful THRESHING FLOOR (**7**; **1h20min**). (From here one can climb to the top of either **Roque de los Brezos**

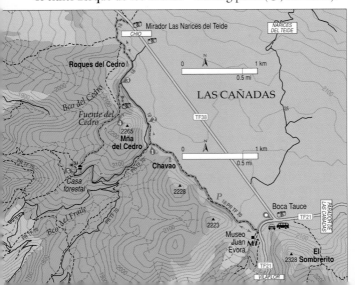

Walk 6: CHAVAO TRAIL AND FIRE-WATCH TOWER

See map opposite; see also photograph page 10

Distance: 8.4km/5.2mi; 2h50min

Grade: ●: relatively easy, with 210m/700ft of ascent overall — but the pumice underfoot is ankle-twisting. National Park trail 18. A short stretch of path requires a head for heights.

Equipment: hiking boots, long trousers, sunhat, warm fleece, windproof, gloves, raingear, picnic, water

Access: 🚗: park at Boca Tauce, by the entrance to the Museo Juan Evora and the entrance to 'Sendero 18' (Car tours 1 and 2; 28° 12.802'N, 16° 40.842'W). Or 🚌 to/from the 'Boca Tauce' bus stop (Timetable 4); journey 1h from Los Cristianos. Walk the short way west to the museum.

Short walk: Chavao Trail (7.2km/4.5mi; 2h10min).
● Easy, but ankle-twisting pumice underfoot; equipment, access/return as above. Follow the main walk to the turn-off for Montaña del Cedro (❸). Here keep straight on, passing the **Roques del Cedro**, to the Mirador Narices del Teide on the TF38. Return the same way.

H ere's an easy walk for everyone. It's well known for its profusion of flora, most notably the summer-flowering *tajinaste rojo* (shown on page 42). If you're just out for a stroll, do the Short walk. But the main walk is well worth the time invested: in under three hours you'll cross a lava field and a *cañada* (a sunken plain of gravel), climb to a pass with superb views over the southern corner of Las Cañadas, and briefly head through a pine wood.

Begin the walk just west of **Boca Tauce**, by the parking for the museum and SENDERO 18 (◉). Follow the signposted trail below the MUSEO JUAN EVORA (a small house owned by the goat-herd who was the last inhabitant of the park — worth a visit!). The path descends towards a lava field amidst broom bushes — some 2m/6ft high. Hemmed in between the undulating crater wall on the left and the sea of jagged lava on the right, the way is straightforward. Small piles of stones keep you on course, and green metal signs, 'SENDERO 18', mark the way.

Soon you encounter pines growing out of the crater walls. Sharp pinnacles of rock rise above you. On this side of the crater, the volcanic cone of Pico Viejo commands your attention, while El Teide stands in the background. Soon (**5min**) you'll

be crossing a corner of the lava flow. It's an intriguing sight, but very jagged underfoot. Some minutes off this scoriaceous lava, you pass to the right of a second type of lava, known as *pahoehoe* ('ropey') lava, since it resembles coils of rope. Montaña del Cedro is now not far ahead. You cross a *cañada* and then pass by the foot of a large rock covered in orange and green lichen (**Chavao; 40min**) — from which the trail takes its name.

Just past this rock, you'll see a track above you, descending the crater wall. On your return you will be re-entering the crater through this pass. Keep to the right here (❶), alongside the wall of the crater (*briefly leaving Sendero 18*); a faint track comes underfoot; it soon becomes well defined. Five minutes from Chavao, step over a wire rope (that prevents vehicle access),

and join the track descending from the pass (**❷**). Now back on Sendero 18, follow it to the right. Less than 10 minutes along (**50min**), at a point where the track curves to the right, leave it: turn left (**❸**; *again leaving Sendero 18*), to begin the ascent of Montaña del Cedro (CAIRN, PAINT DOTS). *(Those doing the Short walk should, however, remain on the track/Sendero 18. Five minutes further on you will pass near the Roques del Cedro, a brilliant amphitheatre of taginaste rojo, and then reach the TF38 at the Mirador Narices del Teide. Retrace steps to end the walk.)*

Beginning the main walk ascent, you may have to push your way through bushes of broom. Small CAIRNS guide you. The path very quickly bears left to ascend the escarpment, and then becomes clear. A very short stretch of path may prove unnerving for those who have no head for heights. Crossing a PASS (**1h 05min**), you have a stupendous view through pine trees over onto Pico Viejo and its surrounding apron of lava. El Sombrerito is the peak that rises to the right of Boca Tauce, and further along the wall is flat-topped Montaña Guajara (Walk 7).

54

Roques del Cedro

Rounding the flanks of **Montaña del Cedro**, the south-western corner of the island opens up, and a large ravine (**Barranco del Cedro**) slips away below you. On clear days you can see La Gomera and the veins of its ridges. El Hierro lies on the horizon behind it. And the two humps that usually float above the clouds are La Palma. A couple of minutes above the pass, the path forks. Bear right uphill, with PAINT DOTS on rocks marking the way. A minute later you clamber over rocks to reach a spring in a cave, the **Fuente del Cedro** (**❹**). A tiny SHRINE sits in the rock face above it.

Higher up, your trail runs through a light pine wood. Rounding the hillside, a bright-red fire-watch tower comes into sight not far below. Shortly after spotting the tower, the path swings along the ridge towards it. The route may be indistinct at times, but small CAIRNS show you the way. Soon you're standing below the FIRE-WATCH TOWER (**❺**; **1h35min**). When they are stationed here, the forestry guards love to have a chat. If you're lucky (and although it's probably against regulations), they'll probably take you up top to see the fine view.

Heading on, follow the forestry track and, at the junction 10 minutes along, ascend to the left. Around 15 minutes uphill you re-enter **Las Cañadas** (**1h 55min**). From the rim of the crater, follow the path back down to **Chavao**. From here retrace your outgoing path back to **Boca Tauce** (**❻**; **2h50min** — or **3h** in all if you came by bus. Do visit the tiny MUSEUM before leaving!

Walk 7: FOUR WALKS TO THE PAISAJE LUNAR

See also photo pages 32-33

Walk a: PR TF 72 — the most popular circuit to Paisaje Lunar

Distance/time: 7.5km/4.7mi; 2h50min

Grade: ● moderate ascent/ descent of 300m/1000ft; good, waymarked PR/GR paths

Equipment: walking boots, walking pole(s), sunhat, fleece, gloves, windproof, raingear, picnic, plenty of water

Access: ⇌ to/from an info board for the PR TF 72 (28° 10.260'N, 16° 37.195'W); it's 3.5km along the Pista Madre del Agua, a motorable eastbound track from KM66 on the TF21

Walk b: Circuit from Vilaflor

Distance/time: 13km/8mi; 5h

Grade: ● fairly strenuous ascent/ descent of 670m/2200ft; good, waymarked PR/GR paths

Equipment: as Walk a

Access: ⇌ to/from Vilaflor (car park near the church; 28° 9.624'N, 16° 38.219'W). Or 🚌 to/from Vilaflor (Timetables 4, 7); journey time from Los Cristianos 35min

Walk c: Parador — Paisaje Lunar — Vilaflor via Walk a

Distance/time: 16.5km/10.2mi; 5h05min

Grade: ● strenuous and long, with an ascent of 265m/870ft and descent of 1120m/3645ft; good, waymarked PR/GR paths

Equipment: as Walk a

Access: 🚌 to the Parador de las Cañadas (Timetable 4); journey from Los Cristianos 1h15min. Return on 🚌 from Vilaflor (Timetables 4, 7); journey time to Los Cristianos 35min

Walk d: Parador — Paisaje Lunar — Vilaflor via Campa- mento Madre del Agua

Distance/time: 19km/12mi; 6h

Grade: ●❢ strenuous and *very* long, with ascents of 365m/ 1200ft and descents of 1170m/ 3850ft. Mostly good GR/PR paths but recommended for experienced walkers: the descent into Paisaje Lunar is very steep and slippery, the waymarking sometimes hard to follow

Equipment: as Walk a

Access/return: as Walk c

The classic hike to the Paisaje Lunar (the tiny gem of a 'Moon Landscape') is a must for all walkers visiting Tenerife. Its setting is a forest of old Canarian pines. The real Canarian pine is the noble among peasants, and the pines of Vilaflor are renowned for their grandeur. Whether you're a beginner walker or a strong hiker, this walk is a must: just choose the version that suits you best.

Start Walk a at the WALKERS' INFO BOARD (**a**) 3.5km along the **Pista Madre del Agua**. Climb the RED/WHITE/YELLOW- waymarked trail to a fork (**3min**). *Both* forks are signed to Paisaje Lunar; head left here (**❶**; you'll return from the right). The beautifully laid out stone-lined trail passes some terraces on the left, crosses a track, then passes a ruin on the left (CASA MARRU- BIAL; **35min**).

Having crossed a *barranco*, head right at the next two forks, always keeping to the same way- marks. But *leave* the GR 131 at **1h10min** (**❷**): it heads left at a fingerpost *(Walks c and d join here)*. Continue right downhill towards 'PAISAJE LUNAR', still on the YELLOW/WHITE WAYMARKED **PR TF 72**. You pass a FIRST VIEW- POINT, from where there is a much-photographed side-on view of **Los Escurriales** — the **Paisaje Lunar**. A SECOND VIEW- POINT (**❸**; **1h35min**). with full-on view, is rather more difficult to photograph. Soft creams, beiges, yellows, browns and greys saturate these smooth conical sandstone moulds rising like turrets on both sides of the **Barranco de las Aguas**.

From here continue ahead (right) towards '*VILAFLOR*' on the easily seen trail, mostly in descent. You eventually come to a junction where the *PR TF 83* joins from the left (**4**; **2h15min**). Head right towards '*VILAFLOR*', still on the

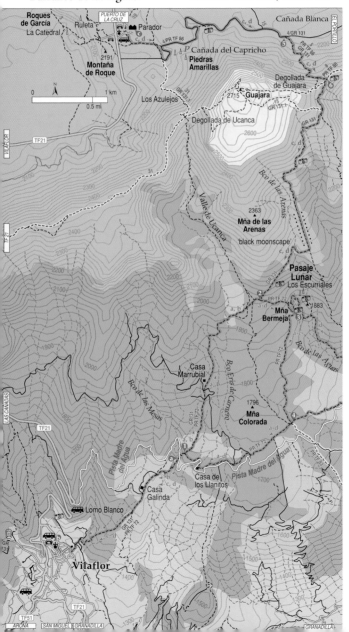

PR TF 72. The trail runs above the **Pista Madre del Agua**, for a while with a high wall on the left. You cross two tracks rising from the *Pista*, pass a ruin (CASA DE LOS LLANITOS), then join the *Pista* itself and follow it round a

Walk d: at the 2h15min-point a large pine provides welcome shade on a hot day, after which rocks flank your route all the way down Montaña de las Arenas (photo looking back uphill).

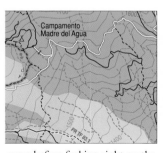

curve before forking right on the trail. You pass the path where you turned left early in the walk (❶) and rejoin the **Pista Madre del Agua** at the WALKERS' INFO BOARD (ⓐ); **2h50min**.
Start Walk b in Vilaflor (ⓑ). From the car park by the church

walk downhill at the left of the PLAZA, then take the third turning left (CALLE EL CANARIO; RED/WHITE/YELLOW WAYMARKS). Turn right at the T-junction; then, 75m downhill, just in front of two large round WATER TANKS, turn left on the signposted trail (**PR TF 72, GR 131**). It drops into a *barranco*, passes another large round WATER TANK and joins a track. Follow this left for 50m, then go sharp right on a walled-in cobbled trail. You rise steeply through pines to a very photo-genic farm set amongst terraces, with an almond grove on the right (CASA GALINDO; **55min**). Pass to the right of the farm and fork half-right through a gap in a wall about five minutes later. Descend into another *barranco*, then rise to the **Pista Madre del Agua** at the point where *Walk a* starts and ends (ⓐ; **1h10min**). Now follow **Walk a**, adding 1h10min to all time checks, and when you return to this point, retrace your steps to **Vilaflor** (ⓑ; **5h**).
Start Walk c at the **Parador de las Cañadas** (ⓒ). Follow NATIONAL PARK TRAIL 4 from the turning circle by the building. Your destination is the prominent mountain protruding out of the crater wall southeast of the Parador. In under 10 minutes the trail takes you to a tarred lane. Straight across is National Park Trail 31; ignore it and turn left to continue east along TRAIL 4. A fascinating formation of pink and yellow rocks rises in front of you. The pastel colours give this fine natural sculpture its name — **Piedras Amarillas** ('Yellow Stones'). Behind them, you cross two small *cañadas* (gravel plains). **Guajara** — the bastion of the encircling walls — is seen at its best, rising 500m/ 1640ft from the crater floor.

Your ascent begins five minutes beyond a turn-off to the left (National Park Trail 15). Here you join the **GR 131** and various other trails (**5**; **50min**) to begin the ascent. Turn right uphill (RED/WHITE/YELLOW WAYMARKS). You reach the edge of the crater at a pass with magnificent views, the **Degollada de Guajara** (**6**; 2373m/7785ft; **1h30min**). Gran Canaria seems surprisingly close from this vantage point. Ignore trails left and right. After a brief ascent, the **GR 131** forks (by a METAL POLE; **1h40min**). The right fork is the main ascent route to Guajara; keep left for Paisaje Lunar. Barely a minute down, the path forks again: keep right with the **GR 131**. Over to your right (still in the distance) is **Montaña de las Arenas**, with its charred sides and maroon summit. Below you, pines full of character dot the landscape. The path turns down a low side-ridge. You pass a large PINE TREE (**2h15min**) — a cool resting place. Minutes below it, you're trudging straight down across the gravelly black sand. Rocks flank your route all the way downhill.

Just before the end of the sand-hill and the first pines, the trail forks. Ignore the path straight ahead down the hill; go right, towards a large pine. Beyond the pine, scramble down a steep, gravelly bank — probably on all fours. You cross the **Barranco de las Arenas** (where you could make a short detour back up the riverbed to a black 'moon landscape').

From the floor of this ravine you ascend a gravelly ridge at the edge of another, lower ravine — the **Barranco de las Aguas**, home of the Paisaje Lunar. From this path you enjoy a first view down into the 'moon landscape'.

When you come to a crossing trail, turn left downhill on the WHITE/YELLOW WAYMARKED **PR TF 72**, joining **Walks a and b** at **2** (**2h50min**). Use the notes for **Walk a** from the **1h10min**-point, adding 1h40min to all times. You come to the SECOND VIEWPOINT (**3**) in **3h15min**. Now keep following Walk a until it ends at the parking place on the **Pista Madre del Agua** (**a**). Then, referring to the map, keep to the RED/WHITE/YELLOW WAYMARKS down to **Vilaflor** (**b**; **5h05min**).

Start Walk d at the **Parador de las Cañadas** (**c**). Follow **Walk c** to the SECOND VIEWPOINT (**3**; **3h15min**). Here you *leave* the PR trail and head back the way you came. You come to a junction where the Paisaje Lunar is signed down to the right. Descending carefully, you're soon walking along the very edge of the **Paisaje Lunar**. At another path junction, head right, alongside the **Barranco de las Aguas**. Crossing a crest, you encounter a WATER PIPE, and minutes later you rejoin the left fork, heading right.

When you meet a track, follow it to the right: a minute downhill, a picturesque CAMPSITE comes into view through the pines. Cut down through the camp, keeping straight downhill, and in a couple of minutes you'll reach the front entrance to **Campamento Madre del Agua** (**3h 45min**). There's a water tap just above the office, to the right of the gate. Just over 200m below the entrance, turn right on a trail running above the **Pista Madre del Agua**. Follow this to the JUNCTION OF THE PR TF 72 AND PR TF 83 (**4**). Keep ahead on the **PR TF 72**, once again following **Walk c**, to descend to **Vilaflor** (**b**; **6h**).

Distance: 5km/3mi; 2h50min
Grade: ●꠱ moderate, with
ascents/descents of some
400m/1300ft overall (almost
continual ups and downs), on
very rocky terrain. You must be
sure-footed and have a head for
heights, and don't attempt in
wet or windy weather. Cairns
and some orange waymarks
Equipment: walking boots,
sunhat, fleece, raingear, windproof, picnic, plenty of water
Access: 🚗: park at the Mirador
de Masca on the TF436 west of
Santiago del Teide (28° 18.018'N,
16° 49.598 'W) — the third parking
west of Santiago. Or 🚌
(Timetable 8) at 09.50 to
Santiago del Teide, to connect
with 🚌 355 from Santiago to
Masca (not in the timetables;
recheck all times in advance):
departs at 11.00 and 13.10;
returns 16:15, 18.25; journey
time 10min. Ask to alight at the
Mirador de Masca: it's *not* an
'official' stop, so for the return,
be sure to *flag down* the bus
opposite the *mirador*
**Alternative walk: Finca de
Guergues** (7km/4.3mi; 4h). ●
Grade, equipment, access as main

walk, but this hike is fairly strenuous, with ascents/descents of
600m/1970ft overall; the path is
sometimes vague and more
slippery (walking poles useful!).
Follow the main walk to **La
Cabezada** (❸; **1h25min**), then
descend the path to the left of
the THRESHING CIRCLE. Pass a
CISTERN built into the hillside a
minute downhill; immediately
beyond it, the path veers off to
the right. *Pay close attention to the
cairns/waymarks from here on.*
About 15 minutes down you
reach **Los Pajares** (❹), a lone
house on a jutting rock. Your
route swings to the right above
the house and descends to the
right of another THRESHING
FLOOR. Remain on the right-
hand side of the steep valley wall.
You pass to the right of another
WATER TANK and come almost at
once to the beautifully sited
Finca de Guergues (❺; **1h
55min**) with its splendid views.
(Not enough? You *could* even
walk on past the *finca* — eventually pathless — to a couple of
VIEWPOINTS over Masca's valley.
Allow 2h05min to return to the
TF436 (**4h**) from Guergues.

H ere's an opportunity to see the Masca Valley without
the exertions of Walk 9. This hike offers spectacular
views as you wind along a high jagged neck of land.
Barrancos fall away on either side, hundreds of metres
below. On the left lies the Barranco Seco del Natero, its
slopes carpeted in shades of green; on the right the
Barranco de Masca is concealed below precipitous walls.

Start out on the TF436 about
150m southwest of the MIRADOR
DE MASCA, at the chained off
track to the farmstead of **Araza**
(○). Take the footpath just to
the right of the track. Six-seven
minutes downhill, on a SADDLE
(❶), ignore the path off left into
the Barranco Seco del Natero.
Crossing bedrock — rich red,

rose, maroon and brown — the
way is at times vague, but bits of
old trail keep appearing (watch,
too, for the CAIRNS and WAY-
MARKS). Yellow-flowering
broom and glossy green-leafed
tabaiba brighten the hillsides.
After passing through a GATE,
you are soon enjoying views
down into *both* ravines, as you

59

View east over the Barranco Seco del Natero, from the threshing floor at Los Pajares (Alternative walk).

stride along the backbone of the ridge. The path dips across a narrow neck of rock. Slowly, the southern coastline unravels from Los Gigantes to Los Cristianos, with the mountains visited on Walks 2-5 rising inland.

As the trail moves briefly to the right-hand side of the ridge and the terrain drops away abruptly, some people may find a short (10m) stretch of path unnerving. The views over the Barranco de Masca are superb. But the sheer-sided peak ahead blocks out everything else for the moment, leaving you wondering: what lies beyond it?

Reaching the *HIGHEST POINT OF THE TRAIL* (❷; 1025m/3360ft), the least expected sight appears: green terraced slopes. A couple of stone huts nestle on the hillside not far below to your right — an exhilarating sight. In just a few minutes you're at the houses

at the top end of the high meadow, **La Cabezada** (❸; **1h25min**). A large CIRCULAR STONE-LAID FLOOR, once used for threshing the wheat and barley that was grown here, sits above the dwellings. This setting, high on the edge of a rocky ridge, commands breathtaking views of the rest of this upheaval of basalt. But for the twitter of a few birds and the distant bleating of goats, the valleys are deathly quiet. La Gomera is clearly visible due south. The tiny hamlet below, precariously perched at the edge of the Barranco Seco del Natero, is the **Finca de Guergues** (❺; Alternative walk).

Returning to the TF436, your views stretch all the way back to El Teide. Be sure to *flag your bus down above* the Araza track, well off the bend, opposite the Mirador de Masca (**2h40min**).

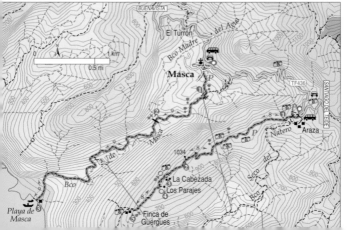

Walk 9: BARRANCO DE MASCA

See map opposite; see also
photograph on page 14
Distance: 9.6km/6mi; 6h
Grade: ● :: very strenuous,
potentially hazardous descent/
ascent of 630m/2070ft; only for
very experienced hikers. You
must be sure-footed and have a
head for heights. Do not attempt
in wet or windy weather!
Equipment: walking boots, sunhat, walking pole(s), raingear,
fleece, windproof, whistle, swimwear, plenty of water, picnic
Access: 🚍: park on the TF436
west of Masca, in one of the
designated car parks (28° 18.357'N,
16° 50.419 'W). These 'official' car
parks fill up quickly; *arrive early!*
Or 🚍 as Walk 8, page 59. You
must catch the 11.00 bus from
Santiago to complete the walk in
time for the 18.25 return bus
from Masca.

**Shorter walk: From Masca to
the weir and back** (2.5km/
1.6mi; 2h15min). ● : Strenuous
descent/ascent of 200m/650ft.
Equipment, access as main walk.
Follow the main walk to the
WEIR; return the same way.
**Alternative walk: Masca —
Playa de Masca** (4.8km/3mi;
2h45min). ● :: Grade, equipment, access as main walk, but
this walk is all descent. Take the
🚍 to Masca (as above), and for
the return pre-arrange for a
Masca–Los Gigantes cruise ⛴
to collect you at the beach (tel:
922 861918 or 922 867049).
*These boats only run when the sea is
calm! Double-check* days and
times of sailings (usually at
13.30, 15.30, 16.30, 18.30),
*and make sure you have a voucher
or ticket.* Follow the main walk to
the jetty at **Playa de Masca**.

The Barranco de Masca lies hidden in the huge block
of roughly-dissected basalt that covers the northwestern corner of the island. It's one of Tenerife's most
popular trails — despite being tough — and easily reached
from a base in the south. Sheer jagged walls — in places
just a few metres apart — rise above a boulder-strewn floor,
leaving the walker only just enough space to squeeze
through, as the *barranco* drops 620m (2035ft) from the
village of Masca to the sea.

Start out at the BUS STOP or one
of the OFFICIAL CAR PARKS on the
TF436 (○). Walk into Masca
village on the stone-paved lane
that passes to the left of the
CHURCH. Just below the square,
turn right on a paved path. A
beautiful descent follows, with
multi-coloured bougainvillaea
billowing out over the walls. The
village has been prettily mani-
cured, with stone walls, stone-
laid paths and stone houses. A
couple of minutes down, you're
in a lower part of the village, on
the ridge between the Barranco
de Masca to the left and the

Barranco Madre del Agua to the
right. Here the lane you first
followed curves in front of you
again: follow it to the right.
Some 40m along, a WALKERS'
SIGNBOARD alerts you to your
trail down left into the **Barranco
de Masca.** A steep, very slippery
descent follows.
The *barranco* is a contrast of
dramatic rock forms and verdant
scenery; at the outset, the slopes
are littered with palms. Reaching
a DYKE in the valley wall, the
path forks: you can go either
side of the dyke. Ahead, the
barranco walls rear up vertically.

61

In the Barranco de Masca —
*approaching the rock arch that is a
popular motif for photographers*

At a SIGN ('ESPACIO NATURAL PROTEJIDO'; **10min**) the trail veers off to the left. When you come face to face with an enormous boulder, circle to the left of it. A very steep, vertiginous descent follows, and you soon cross a WOODEN BRIDGE (❶; **25min**). The trail heads left uphill from the bridge, but quickly curves right, rounding a sheer escarpment: this vertiginous spot requires negotiation on all fours. The *barranco* floor is choked with cane, and you'll probably be surprised to find terracing even on these precipitous walls.

Three more barranco crossings bring you to a LOW WEIR, where the **Barranco Madre del Agua** comes in from the right (❷; **55min**). *The Shorter walk turns back here* but, first, some exploring! *Carefully* scramble up the slippery rock on the right, into the Barranco Madre del Agua. Hidden in amongst the rock and cane lies a deliciously cool, thigh-deep pool.

A narrow IRRIGATION CHANNEL begins at this confluence, built into the left-hand wall of the Barranco de Masca — which now becomes a narrow shaded chasm and veers left towards the sea. Descend the FLOOD WALL on the left. Cross the river bed and, from here on, you can't possibly get 'lost' for more than a minute or two as you weave your way through this maze of rock. To reach the beach from here takes another 90 minutes' clambering over rocks and boulders, maybe ankle-deep wading (depending on rainfall, irrigation requirements, and the season) and climbing *up* old, crumbled paths. You won't have time to read detailed instructions, so none are given (there are some CAIRNS). The indented craggy walls rise precipitously above you — in some places as high as 700m/2300ft. Several small pools add to the cool freshness of the *barranco*.

Eventually you're on a stony beach, the **Playa de Masca** (❸; **2h30min**), probably looking out to a flotilla of tourist boats anchored off the shore. The private house here is by no means an eyesore; its stone blends in with the landscape, and the enclosure full of trees enlivens the mouth of the valley. Depending on the tide, there may be a sandy beach over to the left. But the small jetty over to the right makes an ideal swimming and picnicking spot. Refresh yourself for the uphill slog. Allow an *extra* hour for the return the **Masca** (◯; **6h**).

Walk 10: BARRANCO DE ARURE

Distance: 2.8km/1.7mi; 2h
Grade: ● moderate, with an ascent of just under 200m/650ft. You must be sure-footed and agile: most of the hike is up the *barranco* bed, clambering over and around rocks. Avoid after heavy rain, when the stream bed may not even be negotiable. Waymarked with arrows, dots and wiggly 'water' designs.
Equipment: walking boots, sunhat, fleece, picnic, water
Access: 🚌 or 🚐 (Timetables 11, 16) to/from Casa de la Seda; journey time from Valle Gran Rey 10min. Park in the long roadside car park between El Guro and Casa de la Seda (28° 6.441'N, 17° 19.546'W).

Alternative start via El Guro
(3.4km/2.1mi; 2h15min); grade, equipment, access as main walk. Start 10m below the northern end of the ROADSIDE CAR PARK: opposite the parking and just a few metres below the 'EL GURO' sign (**1**), cross the river on a BRIDGE with iron railings. This walkway rises into **El Guro**, mostly on steps. When it flattens out and forks, go sharp right. Once outside the houses, you pass an impressive wall of basalt prisms on the left, then come to another fork: go left, slightly uphill, and then down into the stream bed — probably on all fours. You join the main walk here at (**3**).

The Barranco de Arure, an idyllic offshoot of the Barranco Valle Gran Rey, is the equivalent of Tenerife's Barranco del Infierno. Both lie in deep rocky ravines, and both boast a decent-sized (for the Canaries, anyway) waterfall. This walk is one big, fun Indiana Jones agility test: scramble over rocks, boulders and fallen tree trunks, creep through dense vegetation and pull yourself up on lianas and branches. Great fun for young and old, but you have to be agile!

The hike starts at the northern (**Casa de la Seda**) end of the long ROADSIDE CAR PARK (**0**), where the bus also stops. Walk north up the road towards Los Granados. Just as the road kinks to the right (and immediately after a garage with some vines on top) take the concrete and stone walkway ascending to the left, the 'CAMINO BARRANCO LOS ANCONES' (**2**). Behind the first house, your route suddenly swings right up the rocky hillface; arrows and dots on a stone wall indicate the turn-off. You circle above the valley floor, which is full of fruit trees and garden plots. Three minutes from the road, at a faint fork, keep left on the lower path.

Severe, dark, jagged basalt walls rise above you, a sharp contrast to the verdant valley floor.
Soon you enter the bed of the **Barranco de Arure** (**5min**) and follow it to the right. From here the route lies mainly in the stream bed. A number of other paths criss-cross the valley floor , including the path from El Guro used in the Alternative walk which comes in from the left behind you at (**3**). Clumps of papyrus grass grow along the stream bed, which contains only a trickle of water at this stage. At times the way is through a corridor of Indian cane. Higher up, stringy willows begin to appear.

63

*Above: the Salto del Agua;
left: alternative start from El Guro*

The course of the river changes
every year after heavy rainfall,
and the amount of water varies
with the seasons. There may be
side paths up the banks at times
to avoid difficult passages, or
there may be small scrambles
next to miniature waterfalls,
sometimes with the help of a
rope or a makeshift ladder. But
for most of the time the way
follows the *barranco* bed. The
higher you rise, the more water
the stream carries and eventually
the sound of gurgling water is all
around you until, finally, you
reach the foot of a 15m/50ft-
high waterfall, the **Salto del
Agua**, in a cool dark rock
cauldron (❹; **1h**).
Allow an hour to retrace your
steps from here to your car or
bus at **Casa de la Seda** (❍; **2h**).

Walk 11: FROM VALLE GRAN REY TO ARURE

See map opposite; see also
photograph page 69
Distance: 8km/5mi; 3h15min
Grade: ● very strenuous, with
an overall ascent of 800m/
2600ft. You must be sure-
footed. Red-white waymarked
(GR 132). *Tip: see Walk 12 to do
the walk as a descent from Arure.*
Equipment: walking boots,
fleece, windproof, sunhat, raingear, picnic, plenty of water
Access: on foot or 🚐 to La
Calera (Timetables 11, 16) or
⛴ to Vueltas (Timetable 18),
then on foot to La Calera.
Return on 🚐 from Arure
(Timetables 11, 16); journey
time to Valle Gran Rey 35min.
***Alternative walk: La Mérica
from Arure*** (7km/4.3mi;
2h25min). ● Quite easy

ascent/descent of 100m/330ft;
equipment as above. Access: 🚐
or 🚐 (Timetables 11, 16)
to/from Arure. The walk proper
starts on the lane to the **Mirador
Ermita del Santo** (❼), which
turns west off a hairpin bend in
the main road. By car, park
opposite Casa Conchita (❽) in
the centre (28° 8.129'N,
17° 19.074'W) and walk 500m
downhill to the turn-off on your
right. By bus, alight at the Bar-
Restaurant El Jape (❾) and walk
north along the road, past the
Las Hayas turn-off, to the first
turning left. This tarmac lane
reverts to track after 200m. Use
the map opposite to follow the
GR 132 to the TRIG POINT on the
La Mérica summit (❺); return
the same way.

Th   his walk scales the precipitous rock walls that over-
shadow La Calera and then heads north. The really fit
will start out from Valle Gran Rey early in the morning
and watch the sun creep slowly over the *barranco* below.
Those who prefer a more leisurely approach can descend
the well-graded route from Arure. Climbing or descending, your views dip into every nook and cranny of the Gran
Rey ravine and out over the desolate southwest.

Start out at the BUS STOP/TAXI
RANK (○) on the GM1 in **La
Calera**, 100m north of the
roundabout. Take the wide steps
(CALLE EL CONTERO) at the left of
the *ayuntamiento* (town hall,
with flags), then the first steps
on the right. At the top of the
steps turn right along a narrow
alley between houses, then turn
left when you meet a road higher
up (on a bend).
Leave this road just beyond a
small BRIDGE and above a large
WATER TANK: a **GR 132** FINGER-
POST marks the start of the walk
proper (❶; **10min**). Take the
stone-laid steps left uphill beside
the stepped *barranco* and swing
left almost immediately to cross

it. Your ascent of the towering
cliffs has begun. This initial
stretch of path, on well-graded
zigzags, is paved in places, but
sometimes very gravelly with
loose grit and small stones. From
here on, always follow the main
red/white waymarked GR,
ignoring any turn-offs.
As you climb, banana plantations, a deep blue sea, and dark
bluffs come into view below —
followed by a glimpse of the
small *barrios* (urban districts)
occupying the highest corner of
the valley, a shrill patch of
greenery in these monochro-
matic surroundings. The island
back across the sea, more than
likely under cloud, is El Hierro.

65

by a cluster of rocks. Soon the country villages of Chipude, El Cercado and Las Hayas (from right to left) come into view, settings for Walks 15, 16 and 18-23.

Five minutes later (**2h15min**) you pass a few paths forking left (**❹**) to the summit of **La Mérica** (**❺**). You cross over a neck of ridge and now briefly catch a view northwest, towards a formidable landscape of bare rock, devoid of life and drained of colour ... the perfect site for a rubbish tip! La Palma lies before you, two rounded peaks emerging above a cape of lingering cloud.

On reaching a TRACK (**❻**; **2h 35min**), continue along it, ignoring the turn-off left to the RUBBISH TIP a few minutes later. Less than 20 minutes along the track, ignore a path on the left signposted to Taguluche (**❹**; the return route for Walks 13 and 14). Just beyond the turn-off, you're gazing down onto Taguluche — a patchwork of gardens in a tremendously deep basin.

A solid slog lasting well over an hour brings you to a RIDGE, from where you look straight down onto La Playa and Vueltas (Valle Gran Rey's port area). This setting is dramatised by the jagged ridges tumbling down alongside you (**Riscos de la Mérica**). Later you reach the CREST (**1h45min**), where goats graze on the remains of terracing. You pass a couple of paths off left to the edge of the Riscos — another fine viewpoint.

Ten minutes later you walk between a RUIN on the left and huge circular THRESHING FLOOR on the right (**❷**; **1h55min**). Continue up the gently sloping terraces, to catch sight of Arure, set back in a shallow gully on the edge of the plateau. About 15 minutes past the threshing floor you pass to the left of a CISTERN and another RUINED HOUSE (**❸**)

Having crossed the ridge a few times, you descend to a tarmac lane. Follow this for 100m, then turn left on a cobbled path to the **Mirador and Ermita del Santo** (**❼**; **3h10min**), a magnificent viewpoint overlooking the Taguluche ravine, setting for Walks 13 and 14 which descend from here to Taguluche.

From the *mirador,* go back to the lane junction and turn left to the main road. Head left uphill to the restaurant CASA CONCHITA in **Arure** (**❽**). Or walk downhill to the Bar-Restaurant EL JAPE (**❾**). In either case you'll reach a BUS STOP (**3h15min**).

Walk 12: FROM ARURE TO VALLE GRAN REY

See photographs opposite and on page 69

Distance: 8km/5mi; 2h25min

Grade: ● moderate, with an overall ascent of 100m/330ft and descent of 800m/2600ft. You must be sure-footed. Red and white waymarking (GR 132).

Equipment: walking boots, fleece, windproof, sunhat, rain-gear, picnic, plenty of water

Access: 🚐 to the Bar-Restaurant El Jape in Arure (Timetables 11, 16); journey time from Valle Gran Rey 35min. Return on 🚐 from La Calera (Timetables 11, 16) or ⛴ from Vueltas (Time-table 18)

Alternative walk: La Mérica (7km/4.3mi; 2h25min). ● See Alternative walk 11 on page 65.

This walk from Arure to Valle Gran Rey will be welcomed by those with strong knees but who don't like the huff and puff of ascents (Walk 11). This descent is steep, but very well graded. I think it's a better way to take in the spectacular views too! Only the 'bare bones' of the route are given here; see Walk 11 for more description.

Start out at the Bar-Restaurant EL JAPE in **Arure** (○). Walk north uphill on the GM1 for 400m, then turn left to the **Mirador and Ermita del Santo** (❶). From the *mirador*, go back to the junction and turn right along the road (then track), soon passing a path off right to Tagu-luche (❷) and, later, a track off right to a RUBBISH TIP. Some 250m past the rubbish tip track, turn right on a **GR 132**-signed path (❸; **25min**).

This broad trail is easily followed. Turn right at (❹; **50min**) and climb to the TRIG POINT on **La Mérica** (❺), then return to the main trail. Further south you first pass a cluster of rocks on the left with a RUINED HOUSE and a CISTERN (❻), then a RUIN on the right and huge circular THRESHING FLOOR on the left (❼; **1h15min**).

Ten minutes later, at a junction, ignore the path off right to the Riscos de la Mérica; keep left for the zigzagging descent — steep but not *too* hard on the knees and *not* vertiginous. Ignore all turn-offs. Eventually the trail emerges at **GR 132** FINGERPOSTS (❽). Turn right and follow the

lane for 250m; then, after a hairpin bend to the left, bear right down to a BUS STOP/TAXI RANK on the GM1 in **La Calera**. The BUS STATION is to the left of the roundabout (❾; **2h25min**).

Walk 13: TAGULUCHE CIRCUIT VIA THE GR 132

See map overleaf
Distance: 11km/6.8mi; 4h
Grade: ● ❗ very strenuous —
especially the return ascent of
700m/2300ft. Overall descent/
ascent 850m/2750ft. The long
descent follows some skiddy,
partly vertiginous paths; you
must be sure-footed and have a
head for heights. Only attempt
in good weather! Parts of the
walk are waymarked (red/white
GR 132; later Sendero 8).
Important note: Several maps
and guides feature a footpath in
the Barranco de Guaranet north
of Taguluche (called Barranco de

Guariñén on some maps). I do
not recommend this path: it is in
extremely poor condition and
will no longer be maintained by
the government, as it is no
longer one of their 40 recommended walks (see page 34).
Equipment: walking boots,
walking pole(s), fleece, windproof, long trousers, whistle,
sunhat, picnic, plenty of water
Access: 🚗 to Arure; park
opposite Casa Conchita in the
centre (28° 8.129'N, 17° 19.074'W).
Or 🚐 to Arure (Timetables 11,
16); alight at the Bar-Restaurant
El Jape.

I f you like challenging hikes in barren and impressive
landscapes, then this is the walk for you! The terrain is
rugged and harsh, but the scenery is spectacular. The route
starts off along 'cliff-hanging' paths, and the homeward
stretch is a marvel — the path coils its way up a sheer valley
wall, yet never once is it vertiginous.

Start out in **Arure**. If you come
by car, from CASA CONCHITA
(●) walk 500m downhill
towards Valle Gran Rey, to a
hairpin bend in the main road,
where you can turn right for the
MIRADOR ERMITA DEL SANTO. If
you come by bus, alight at the
bus stop outside the Bar-
Restaurant EL JAPE (ⓐ) and
follow the main road towards
the centre of Arure, passing the
Las Hayas turn-off. Then take
the first left turn off the hairpin
bend for the MIRADOR ERMITA
DEL SANTO. After 100m turn
right to climb a paved walkway,
the red/white-waymarked
GR 132, to the **Mirador Ermita
del Santo** (❶). From here, the
dramatic setting of Taguluche,
500m/1650ft below, sets the
mood for the hike. Take your
bearings here: you will head
along the escarpment to the
right and then descend, to circle
in front of the razor-like ridge on

the right side of the valley — at
the end of which lies the chapel
shown overleaf. The return route
is up the left wall of the
Taguluche Valley.
Still keen? Set off on the GR
path behind the *ermita* and, after
50m, keep right at a Y-fork
(Walk 14 goes left here). Make
your way through a light
scattering of pines, to edge along
the escarpment. The views are
stupendous — for those sure
enough of foot to enjoy them. A
very steep descent (initially on a
stone-paved path) follows but,
some 20 minutes from the
mirador, a section of path, below
vertical rock walls, is very loose
underfoot, narrow and
vertiginous.
You reach the edge of a VAST
BASIN (**40min**), looking down
on the large farming settlement
of Alojera. The heights,
benefiting from the trade winds,
are noticeably greener than the

The large, beautifully designed Mirador de la Ermita del Santo overlooks Taguluche at the start of the walk; see also photos on pages 1, 31 and overleaf.

lower hills, some of which are totally bare.

Another slippery, gravelly descent drops you down over the ridge towards the Taguluche road. Just before you reach the road, turn sharp left at a fork (❷; **1h**), *leaving* the GR 132 which continues on the far side of the road to Alojera. The well-kept path overlooks the desolate and inhospitable **Barranco de Guaranet**. (Originally this walk approached Taguluche via the Guaranet *barranco*, but the path has deteriorated badly in recent years — extremely narrow and exposed, in some places it's almost invisible; since it is not on the Cabildo's list of recommended walks, it is unlikely ever to be repaired.)

Five minutes along you cross a crest — to find the tiny settlement of Taguluche now lying at your feet in the depth of the next *barranco*. The path is lined with *Euphorbia*, wild flowers and agaves.

When you reach the Taguluche road, cross it and pick up the downhill trail again (10m to the left and cairn-marked). Meet the end of a road near a small CEMETERY (❸) and cross it to continue downhill. When you come to a WATERCOURSE (❹; **1h20min**), walk along the right-hand side for a minute, then cross over to the left side and walk uphill. Just before you reach the MAIN ROAD (by a WATER DEPOSIT; ❺), pick up an old track and follow it to the right. Soon it becomes a path and turns right downhill through an old palm grove, back to the road. Now follow the road to the right, downhill. At the next junction turn right uphill to the pretty **Ermita Virgen del Buen Viaje** (❻; **1h50min**), where you can enjoy a break in the shade.

Setting off again, walk back to the junction with the main road and now turn right. Ignore a road to the right just past Bar-Restaurant Taguluche. In 10 minutes you reach a TURNING AREA at the end of the road (❼; **2h05min**).

From the turning area go back along the road for about 20m, then climb signposted steps on the right, which leads into an old

69

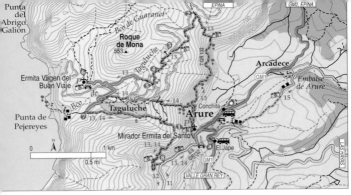

trail. Barely a minute up (just past the last house), turn left on a narrow path climbing the hillside (WHITE ARROW). A couple of minutes up, the old path becomes clearer.

A good five minutes from the road, you cross a three-way water pipe and continue straight up the hillside, ignoring the paths left and right. You're over-looking Taguluche, which clings to the ridge opposite. Small garden plots, green and fertile, occupy most of the ridge, with a mixture of mango, fig, avocado, citrus trees and an abundance of palms. The path is now clearly defined and marked with occasional cairns.

The path crosses to the left of the valley floor (**2h30min**); 50m further on, ignore a path to the left. On the outskirts of **Taguluche**, ascend through abandoned terracing, after 15 minutes ignoring a path to the right. With the ascent nearly over (**3h30min**), go through a passage in the ridge top — to overlook an abyss. A minute later, the path loops up below a goat's pen. Ten minutes further uphill, you join a TRACK and turn left (this is the red/white waymarked **GR 132**; ❽). After 10 more minutes, pass the turn-off to the Mirador Ermita del Santo and reach the road in **Arure**. Turn right to the BUS STOP outside the Bar-Restaurant EL JAPE (ⓐ) — or turn left if you've parked near the CASA CONCHITA (O; **4h**).

Taguluche's Ermita Virgen del Buen Viaje (also called Ermita San Juan de Dios) is the most peaceful, splendid place for a picnic break, beautifully shady and with splendid views out to sea and up to the cliffs, with the Mirador Ermita del Santo on the heights above.

Walk 14: TOUGH TAGULUCHE CIRCUIT

See map opposite; see also
photos pages 1, 31 and 69
Distance: 8.6km/5.3mi; 3h45min
Grade: ● ‼ very strenuous
descent of 620m/2030ft down a
very steep, exposed path. You
must be sure-footed and have a
head for heights. Only suitable
in fine weather, and only for very
experienced hikers. *Danger of*
rockfall, especially in wet weather!
Equipment: walking boots,
walking pole(s), fleece, windproof, long trousers, whistle,
sunhat, picnic, plenty of water
Access: 🚐 to Arure; park opposite Casa Conchita in the centre
(28° 8.129'N, 17° 19.074'W). Or 🚌
to the Bar-Restaurant El Jape in
Arure (Timetables 11, 16)

An alternative to Walk 13, this trail — which dives
straight down to Taguluche — has recently been
cleared and improved, but it is still *very* steep and vertiginous. You *could* do it the other way round, ascending
from Taguluche, but the most challenging section is at the
top. If you were to find that you couldn't manage it, you
would have to go all the way back down to Taguluche…

Start out by following **Walk 13**
on page 68 to the **Mirador**
Ermita del Santo (**1**). Then
continue on the red/white-
waymarked **GR 132**. But after
only 50m, where the Walk 13
continues to the right, turn off
left (FINGERPOST). This narrow
path drops down the face of the
escarpment, often on steep steps.
Check your vertigo tolerance
here: this is the most precipitous
part of the walk. The views are
magnificent throughout, but *stop*
to enjoy them!
Some 30 minutes below the
mirador, you pass just to the left
of a strip of trees, followed by
some scrambling on a loose

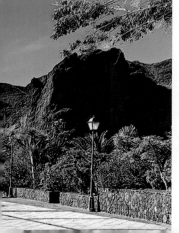

surface. Ten minutes later the
path goes straight down the
ridge, following the line of an
electricity cable.
Lower down, you meet a track.:
follow it to the right for about
150m, through a zig and a zag,
then go left down a walkway to a
bend in the main Taguluche
road. Turn right, then immediately left on a concrete lane in
front of two houses. At a
T-junction, go left on a signed
path, but turn right in front of a
water deposit, down to a
U-bend on the main road (by a
garage). Follow the road downhill for 100m, then turn sharp
left on (signed) Camino de las
Tenerías. In 100m this becomes
a stepped trail that descends past
colourful gardens to the main
road in **Taguluche** (**5**;
1h30min).
Follow the road uphill past Bar-
Restaurante Taguluche, then
take the next left, to the lovely
Ermita Virgen del Buen Viaje
(**6**; **1h35min**) — also know as
Ermita San Juan de Dios and
Ermita San Salvador… Pick up
Walk 13 here at the 1h50min-
point and follow it to the end.

71

Walk 15: ARURE • LAS HAYAS • LOS GRANADOS

See map and photo overleaf
Distance: 9.3km/5.8mi; 3h
Grade: ● relatively easy, with an ascent of 100m/330ft and an overall descent of 850m/2800ft. *But the final 400m/1300ft descent to Los Granados is very steep and tough on the knees.*
Various waymarks, signposts, some cairns
Equipment: walking boots, walking pole(s), sunhat, fleece, windproof, raingear, picnic, water
Access: 🚌 to the El Jape Bar-Restaurant in Arure (Timetables 11, 16); journey time from Valle Gran Rey 35min. Return on the same bus from Los Granados; journey time 10min to Valle Gran Rey

Short walk: From Las Hayas to Los Granados (4.7km/3mi; 1h55min). ● Grade (descent) and equipment as above. Access: 🚌 (Timetables 11, 14, 16) to La Montaña Restaurant (❸) at Las Hayas; journey time 50min. Follow the main walk from the 1h05min-point to the end.

Few walks on this island are without their ups and downs, and most have at least one vertiginous section. But this walk has no long uphill slog, and the vertiginous stretches can be avoided. The gentle climb through a fragment of the laurel wood and the spectacular descent into Valle Gran Rey make this a superb, fairly easy hike — for those with strong knees!

Start out at the Bar-Restaurant EL JAPE (**○**): continue along the road towards **Arure**. But just around the bend in the road, fork right towards Las Hayas. Arure is strung out along the far wall of the valley, while the floor of the *barranco* is crammed with vegetable gardens. A good five minutes uphill, leave the road just above a SMALL RESERVOIR: take the path down to and alongside the dam wall. Beyond the dam wall turn right at the fork. Once past the houses above the dam, follow the path up to the left (northeast) over a rocky ridge; small cairns mark the route. The ridge is covered in yellow-flowering *Tecina linifolia Gomerae*.
Crossing the crest, a view opens up over an elevated valley. The path, rich in mauve, pink, and terracotta hues, joins a track and curves to the right. Tarmac

comes under foot at the first house, the lane passes above a second reservoir (**Embalse de Arure; ❶; 30min**). At a

Valle Gran Rey, from about the 1h30min-point in the walk

72

T-JUNCTION (**35min**) turn right, and at the following Y-fork (where there are many signs) turn right again for 'LAS CRECES', climbing into a basin full of vineyards.

At the next fork, keep right for . 'LAS HAYAS'. Follow the tarred lane uphill until it ends just above a stream bed (**40min**). Cross the *barranco* and ascend a path into a patch of laurel wood. Meeting another ROAD (**❷**; **50min**), turn left. Keeping to the crest of the ridge (**Cabezo de la Vizcaína**), ignore all turn-offs. As you cut through a crest, Las Hayas comes into view, a small scattering of houses surrounded by heather and laurel woods. Approaching the village, a road joins from the right. Five minutes later, just before the main road in **Las Hayas**, go half left uphill on a track and then turn right on a lane, to emerge facing the MONTAÑA RESTAURANT (**❸**; **1h05min**),

described on page 22 and shown on page 75.

From the restaurant, return to the main road, and immediately turn sharp left on a lane (**GR 131**; red and white waymarks). This leads down into a valley of palm trees, crosses a *barranco* and then rises gently. Coming over a low crest, you meet a crossing road (**1h15min**): go straight over but, 25m further downhill, turn left on the **GR 131** (**❹**) and begin to descend into another valley of palms. Then, at a Y-fork 50m further on, *leave the GR:* turn right for 'LA VISCAINA' (**❺**; the GR 131 continues ahead to El Cercado). Cross a track to continue into the valley and, on the far side, at a JUNCTION (**❻**) beyond another low crest, go right— to overlook an abyss, the **Barranco del Agua**, a tributary of the Barranco Valle Gran Rey. From here you can make out the line of a path ascending the valley wall opposite; it climbs to

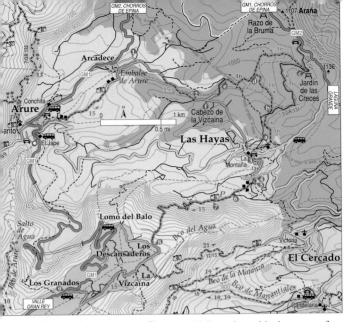

Senecio sp.

Aeonium nobile

Greenovia
aurea

*Ranunculus
cortusfolius*

Taginaste
(Echium
decaisnei)

Peorera
(Andryala
cheiran-
thifolia)

El Cercado and is the route of Walk 21. La Fortaleza, the table-topped rock shown on pages 84-85 (Walk 22), sits in the background. Soon the striking grandeur of Valle Gran Rey, a luxuriant tapestry of banana groves, cane and vegetable gardens, comes into view. A small *mirador* with a stone bench (**7**) makes a fine picnic spot.

Coming onto cobbles (**1h 30min**), you now begin a *very steep* descent down a zigzag path; it's a fine piece of workmanship, and not at all vertiginous. The whole length of the valley lies in view. Cross a small watercourse and keep left at a fork just beyond it, to step down to a road in **Los Descansaderos** (**8**; **2h30min**). Turn left down the palm-flooded valley floor. Keep to this road all the way to the Valle Gran Rey road, ignoring the side road forking to the left. When you reach the main road at **Los Granados** (**9**; **3h**), descend to the BUS STOP, a minute downhill to the left.

Walk 16: JARDIN DE LAS CRECES FROM LAS HAYAS

See map opposite; see also photograph overleaf

Distance: 4km/2.5mi; 1h15min

Grade: ● easy, with an ascent/descent of only about 60m/200ft

Equipment: trainers, fleece, windproof, raingear, water

Access: ⛟ to/from La Montaña Restaurant at Las Hayas (28° 7.759'N, 17° 17.543'E). Or 🚌 (Timetables 11, 14, 16) to La Montaña; journey time 50min

Alternative walk: Extension to the Cabezo de la Vizcaína
(5.3km/3.3mi; 1h35min).

● Quite easy, with an ascent/descent of 150m/490ft. Access, equipment as main walk. At the 50h-point (**d**), continue on the path, along the right-hand side of the gully. When you join a FORESTRY TRACK (**e**), follow it to the left uphill. Soon asphalt

Dona Efigenia's well-known La Montaña restaurant at Las Hayas

comes underfoot. Meeting another road on the **Vizcaína ridge** (**b**), turn left and follow Walk 15 from just past the 50min-point back to La Montaña (**3**; **1h35min**).
NB: Alphabetical waypoints are used for this walk to avoid confusion with Walk 15 on the map.

This little gem of a circuit in a centuries-old, untouched laurel forest, established as a self-guided walk by the National Park authorities, is a brilliant introduction to the *laurisilva* forest, with its mosses, ferns, and creepers.

Start in Las Hayas: from LA MONTAÑA (**3**) walk east uphill on the main road (with the restaurant on your right). In the next curve, turn left on the **GR 131**, passing the entrance to house No 4 on your left; RED/WHITE WAYMARKS). Walk to the left of the village CHURCH (**a**; **5min**), then turn left at a fork and enter the **Garajonay National Park** (SIGNPOST after 20m). At a junction 30m past the sign, keep half right, going through a wind-sculpted part of the laurel

Codeso
(Adenocarpus foliolosus)

Retama
(Spartocytisus supranubius)

forest — the trees are covered with moss and dripping with lichen — very like those in the photo overleaf.

Reaching a wide forestry track with a signpost 'CARRETERA DORSAL' (**b**; **15min**), fork right. In 20min you pass through the little **Jardin de las Creces** picnic area (**c**; **35min**). Now *leave* the GR 131 (which continues ahead to the main road): take the first path to the left (by a 'LAS CRECES' sign), along a small fern-covered gully.

At a JUNCTION (**d**; a little over 15 minutes after leaving the GR 131; **50min**), turn left. Some 15min later (after a bit of a huff and puff) you arrive back at the junction with the CARRETERA DORSAL (**b**; **1h05min**). Cross this track and retrace your steps to **Las Hayas** (**3**; **1h15min**).

Walk 17: RASO DE LA BRUMA CIRCUIT

Distance: 2km/1.2mi; 50min
Grade: ● easy, with a descent/ascent of just 100/330ft
Equipment: trainers, fleece, windproof, raingear, water

Access: 🚌 to/from the Jardín de las Creces turn-off on the GM2 about 1km north of Cruce de Las Hayas (28° 8.578'N, 17° 17.122'W)
Even easier walk (under 2km; 40min). ● Very easy, gentle ups and downs of about 50m/165ft. Access, equipment as main walk. Follow the walk via the viewpoints to **Raso de la Bruma** (❸) and retrace your steps from there.

This very short walk in a fairytale forest is an easy but rewarding introduction to the National Park. It can be shortened to an even gentler stroll, ideal for young and old, and especially suitable as a leg-stretcher on Car tour 6.

Start out at the turn-off to **Jardín de las Creces** on the GM2 (❶); there's a signpost just *inside* the turn-off (not easily seen from the main road — especially in fog!). Park in the small parking area and follow the road north for 100m, then fork right on a National Park-signposted

Trees covered with moss and dripping with lichen

footpath to 'VALLEHERMOSO'. When this forks immediately, go left (❶), rising very gently on the slopes of **Montaña de la Araña** through a Hansel and Gretel forest of moss- and lichen-clad trees.
Two adjacent VIEWPOINTS (❷) come up on the right almost at once, via steps off to the right. On a clear day they offer fine views over Vallehermoso and the north. Further ahead, ignore the trail off to the right (National Park route 12 and your return route); keep ahead to **Raso de la Bruma**, a small picnic area (❸; **20min**). From here retrace your steps for 100m *(or back to the start for the very short walk)*, then fork left. This path rises more steeply on the flanks of Araña, to a junction with the **GR 131** by some rocks, the **Risquillos de Corgo** (❹; **35min**). Alternative walk 42-2 heads northeast from this junction en route from Las Hayas to Vallehermoso. You now follow the GR 131 in the opposite direction, and head south, back to your starting point at the entrance to **Jardín de las Creces** (❶; **50min**).

Walk 18: CHIPUDE • ERMITA NUESTRA SEÑORA DE GUADALUPE • VALLE GRAN REY

Map begins overleaf, ends on page 81; photos pages 79, 80
Distance: 9.7km/6mi; 3h25min
Grade: ● ∷ moderate-strenuous, with a descent of just over 1000m/3300ft. You must be sure-footed and have a head for heights. The descent into Valle Gran Rey is very slippery: don't attempt the walk in wet weather.

Equipment: walking boots, walking pole(s), fleece, wind-proof, sunhat, raingear, picnic, water
Access: 🚐 to Chipude (Time-tables 11, 14, 16); journey time from Valle Gran Rey 1h. Or 🚗: Park in Chipude, off the plaza, and return by bus to your car (Timetables 11, 16).

Leaving Chipude, the highest village on the island (1050m/3450ft), you may well set off in a playful mist; it creeps down on you, then disperses in wisps, revealing picture-postcard views. The walk winds its way through two quiet, green valleys before making a dramatic descent into Valle Gran Rey.

Setting out from the CHURCH in Chipude (○), cross the road to BAR LA CANDELARIA, and descend the lane at the right of the bar (initially cobbled, but it quickly becomes tarred). On reaching the road to El Cercado, turn left. After 25m, turn right down another signposted road. When the road forks after some 50m, keep right. At the end of the road, take steps which descend to a house on the right. Then turn left immediately on a trail with street lights. You leave the last of the houses behind and descend into the valley. Soon meeting a TRACK (❶; **10min**), turn left and then immediately right. After a few minutes keep left at a fork. Fig trees abound in this valley (**Barranco de los Manantiales**), and large tracts of prickly pear cover the *barranco* walls, suggesting earlier cultivation.
Twenty minutes from the track, keep an eye out for the SHARP RIGHT TURN IN THE PATH (❷; **30min**), to continue down into the valley. In about 10 minutes, you arrive at the bed of the **Barranco de la Matanza** (❸;

40min), where you join a trail coming down from El Cercado. *(the return route for Walk 19.)* Almost straight ahead a trail drops very steeply down towards La Vizcaína; it's worth enjoying the FANTASTIC VIEW (ⓐ) at the start of that path.
The main walk continues to the left, following the left-hand side of the Barranco de Argaga. A disused *canal* in varying stages of collapse will keep you company all the way to the Ermita Nuestra Señora de Guadalupe. Most of the time you're walking alongside it on a clear path, sometimes — for very short stretches — you're walking within it. In winter, pretty pools fill the *barranco* bed. A mass of stone walls covers the sides of the valley. The *ermita* comes into sight ahead, sitting on a protruding ridge. Coming into a corner of the *barranco* full of fruit trees, vegetable plots and vines, scramble over and around the broken *canal,* to cross a side *barranco* (**50min**).
Here you need to identify the route you'll be taking after visiting the *ermita*. It's in view

77

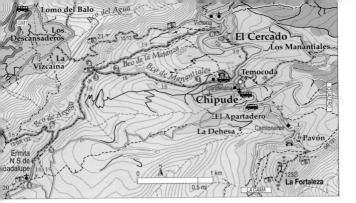

for the next 15 minutes: it is the lower and clearer of two paths ascending the valley wall opposite. Notice, too, the cobbled trail that crosses the canal and descends into the valley, to join this lower path — it's the red/white waymarked GR 132, your ongoing route.

But first visit the chapel, five minutes further along the *canal* — the **Ermita Nuestra Señora de Guadalupe** (④; **1h10min**). The tiny chapel makes an ideal picnic spot, with far reaching views across *barrancos* and out to sea. *(Walk 19 returns to Chipude from this chapel.)*

Return to the crossing with the **GR 132** (⑤) and descend left, *now referring to the map on page 81.* The cobbled trail crosses the bed of the **Barranco de Argaga** (⑥) and then turns back to the left. At a fork higher up, keep left. Ascending to the pass, you look down into the emerald-green pools of the *barranco* bed. Crossing the signposted pass (⑦; **Degollada del Cerrillal**; **1h40min**), keep *right.* (Do not continue along the crest to the left.) Start to descend into Valle Gran Rey. An impressive view greets you straight away, and more views unfold on the descent — of severe, charred-brown ravine walls that seal off the valley. The downhill path is initially in good shape, but

further down steep and gravelly — extremely slippery! *Descend with care!* The enormity of the valley is evident minutes later, when you peer down onto its upper reaches over a mosaic of vivid green plots and palm trees layering the floor, set off by bright-white dwellings. On the descent you pass a makeshift GOATS' PEN (**2h**).

The path twirls steeply downhill, and the rest of the valley opens up. Curling up and over a rocky ridge, you come to two forks: go right at the first one, then, half a minute later, keep left at the next, on a wide cobbled trail. Just after crossing a stream bed, pass two RUSTIC COTTAGES with colourful gardens (⑧; **2h40min**). Turn left at the junction below them, making for another chapel, the Ermita de los Reyes. Keep downhill on the main path. Cross the courtyard of the **Ermita de los Reyes** (⑨; **2h45min**) and descend steps on the right.

Now you can either follow the GR 132 across the *barranco* and up to the main road in **El Guro** (ⓑ; **2h55min**; BUS STOP) or keep on the track until the next right turn. Then join the road and follow it (there is a pavement) to the ROUNDABOUT at **Valle Gran Rey**. Turn left here, to the **La Calera** BUS STATION (ⓒ; **3h25min**).

Walk 19: CIRCUIT FROM CHIPUDE VIA NUESTRA SEÑORA DE GUADALUPE AND EL CERCADO

Map opposite; photo page 80
Distance: 8km/5mi; 2h45min
Grade: ●: relatively easy
circular walk, with a descent/
re-ascent of 300m/1000ft. But
you must be sure-footed and
have a head for heights.
Equipment: walking boots,
walking pole(s), fleece, windproof, sunhat, raingear, picnic,
water
Access: 🚗 to/from Chipude;
park off the plaza (28° 6.595'N,
17° 16.908'W). Or 🚌 to Chipude
(Timetables 11, 14, 16); journey
time from Valle Gran Rey 1h.

*Walks 18 and 19: spring landscape
in the Barranco de los Manantiales*

Nuestra Señora de Guadalupe's balcony-like perch
offers a superb view, looking down into the Barranco
de Argaga as it twists and winds its way seaward. Of the
three walks I describe that visit this delightful bijou
ermita, this is by far the easiest.

Start out at the CHURCH in
Chipude (◯): follow Walk 18
to the **Ermita Nuestra Señora
de Guadalupe** (④), shown
overleaf.
Then return (*past the turn-off
where Walk 18 descends left on
the GR 132 at ⑤*) to the
Barranco de la Matanza, first
encountered at the 40min-point
on your outward walk (❸;
1h40min). Turn left uphill here
on a path signposted for 'EL
CERCADO'. Notice the rocks: on
the opposite site of the *barranco*
they are covered with white
lichen because of the influence
and the direction of the wet
trade winds, while on the other
side of the barranco they are
black, protected from these
prevailing winds.
After some 20 minutes uphill
from the valley floor the trail
enters a side-arm of the valley. El
Cercado is now visible on the

top. You pass through prickly
pear, agaves and many
abandoned terraces. Higher up
the path is lined with small white
rock roses *(Cistus)*. Some 10
minutes later, when the path
forks above cultivated fields,
keep left.
Coming to a road in another five
minutes, turn left; then, 10m
further on, turn right on the
signposted and RED/WHITE WAY-
MARKED **GR 131** for 'CHIPUDE'
(❻; **2h20min**). After 100m you
cross the main road and then
climb the ridge above. When
you cross a track, descend the
hillside on the same path.
Chipude lies across the valley.
Go over the main road once
more and then cross a shallow
valley. Rejoining the main road,
this time follow it to the right,
into **Chipude**. After 350m, turn
left, back to the CHURCH (◯;
2h45min)

Walk 20: BARRANCO DE ARGAGA

Distance: 13km/8mi; 5h50min
Grade: ● ‡‡ very strenuous, with an ascent of 800m/2600ft, often up sheer rock faces (you will need your hands) and along narrow ledges. You must be sure-footed and have a head for heights. Although yellow/white waymarked (it was the old PR LG 14), the path is hard to follow at times. Only recommended in dry weather and for very experienced, adventurous hillwalkers, only on fine days, *and only ascending* (the waymarks are placed for people climbing).
Equipment: walking boots, walking pole(s), fleece, windproof, sunhat, raingear, picnic, water
Access: 🚗 to/from Vueltas (the port at Valle Gran Rey; 28° 4.916'N, 17° 20.000'W). Or 🚐 (Timetables 11, 16) or ⛴ (Timetable 18) to/from Vueltas — or on foot from VGR

T his is arguably the wildest walk on the island — thrilling and exhilarating; the most popular of the island's challenging walks for experienced hillwalkers. But it is *very tough;* make sure you're super-fit and the weather is stable: rockfalls are not uncommon here!

Start out at **Vueltas** (○): follow the track (there may still be a signpost and waymarks for the old PR LG 14) below the

huge mass of **Tequergenche** to **Playa de Argaga**. In front of FINCA ARGAYALL (a holiday and meditation centre) turn left up the track into the **Barranco de Argaga** (❶; **15min**). Shortly after passing Argayall's TROPICAL FRUIT GARDENS, in front of another property, follow the waymarking to the right, into the *barranco* bed. The *barranco* soon narrows (by some concrete foundations), and the waymarks take you left over reddish rocks and alongside a wall, back into the stream bed. Keep right; your initially clear trail quickly starts to climb the *barranco* itself, at the right of a small RESERVOIR. But before long you will be clambering over terraces, crisscrossing the *barranco*, walking pathless over bedrock or using your hands to haul yourself up rock faces. Put the book away, and rely on the waymarks. *Do not forge on until you locate the waymarks ahead.* Two LANDMARKS/TIME CHECKS: TERRACES on the left side of the *barranco* (**1h15min**) and a large ROCK

The Ermita Nuestra Señora de Guadalupe, seen from above Gerián

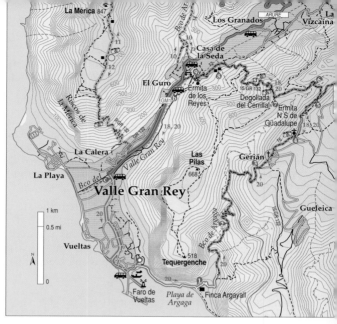

OVERHANG/CAVE (**2**; **1h50min**), with magnificent views back down the *barranco*.

Arriving at **Gerián** (**3**; **3h**), keep to the path at the left of the houses, then join the village road by a SHRINE on the left. Just 40m/yds further along the road, turn left on a wide path that passes between two houses (**GR 132**). Above the second house, cross a *canal* and rise up the crest. The chapel is now in sight. Follow the cobbled trail for two minutes more until it forks, then *leave* the GR 132, keeping straight on (left) on a path to the **Ermita Nuestra Señora de Guadalupe** (**4**; **3h15min**).

From the chapel the circuit is the same as Walk 18: use the notes on page 78. Start by walking north to the crossing with the **GR 132** (**5**) and descending to the left. *(But those not needing to return to their car could shorten the walk by making for Cercado or Chipude: see Walk 19.)*

More LANDMARKS/TIME CHECKS: you recross the **Barranco de Argaga** (**6**) yet again, and reach

a signposted pass, the **Degollada del Cerrillal** (**7**; **3h45min**), where you keep *right* and begin the descent into Valle Gran Rey. The path, initially good, is quite skiddy further downhill, so *descend with care!* On this walk you will be passing the makeshift GOATS' PEN at about **4h05min** and come to the two RUSTIC COTTAGES with gardens (**8**) at about **4h45min**. After crossing the courtyard of the **Ermita de los Reyes** (**9**; **4h50min**), descend steps on the right. Now you can either follow the GR 132 across the *barranco* and up to the main road in **El Guro** (**b**; **5h**; BUS STOP) or keep on the track until the next right turn. Then join the road and follow it (there is a pavement) to the ROUNDABOUT at **Valle Gran Rey**. Turn left here, to the **La Calera** BUS STATION (**c**; **5h 30min**). If you've left a car at the start of the walk, allow another 15-20 minutes via the main street to the parking at **Vueltas** (**o**; **5h50min**).

81

Walk 21: FROM LOMO DEL BALO TO CHIPUDE

Distance: 6km/3.7mi; 2h20min
Grade: ● quite strenuous, with an overall ascent of just under 650m/2130ft, but with no danger of vertigo. Signposting, from El Cercado to Chipude red/white waymarked GR 131
Equipment: walking boots, walking pole(s), sunhat, fleece, windproof, raingear, picnic, water

Access: 🚌 to Lomo del Balo at the end of Valle Gran Rey (Timetables 11, 16); journey from Valle Gran Rey 15min. Return on 🚌 from Chipude (Timetables 11, 14, 16); journey time to Valle Gran Rey 1h
Alternative walk: Combine this with the ascent of La Fortaleza, for a really satisfying day (but note the ●∷ grading!).

I most enjoy this walk in the evening, when the steep valley walls come alive under the setting sun. But if you don't like climbing and want to do the walk as a descent, then chose the morning, with the sun behind you — in the evening the sun will blind you and you won't see a thing.

Leave the bus at **Lomo del Balo** (○), at the TURN-OFF FOR LA VIZCAINA. **Set off** by following the road round the end of the valley to two stepped hamlets, first **Los Descansaderos** (❶) and then **La Vizcaína** (❷; **20min**). Just 20m before house No 71, take the stepped and cobbled path ascending from the parking bay (INFORMATION BOARD and signpost for 'EL CERCADO'). Keep left and walk straight uphill, looking across a lush palm-studded corner of the valley. After a few minutes, ignore a path to the left. Now the cliffs rise straight up in front of you.

Soon you cross a *canal* (IRRIGA-TION CHANNEL; ❸). Ignore the minor paths to the right; you will stay on this main trail all the way to the village of El Cercado. Prickly pear, broom, and *tabaiba* grow out of the hillside rock. The trail, a magnificent piece of workmanship, winds its way up the valley wall, from one ledge to another. Ignore a trail off right (❹; **50min**): it is a very difficult, potentially dangerous ascent. Partridges may startle you, as your passage flushes them out of the bushes. The

barranco soon closes into a narrow defile.

The trail leaves the valley and, mounting a crest, meets a small ROAD by a CEMETERY (❺; **1h40min**). Now walking along the very edge of the valley wall, a spectacular view is revealed down to the left. El Cercado comes into sight, its houses sprinkled around a basin.

Go straight up the road to the main road in **El Cercado** (❻; **1h50min**). Turn right and after 40m reach the Bar-Restaurant VICTORIA, a friendly place with good food.

Descend the concrete path opposite, below the road and BUS STOP, heading left and meandering through this sleepy farming village. On reaching a small road, turn right for 130m, then climb the RED/WHITE WAY-MARKED **GR 131** (❼) to the left. Cross the main road and climb the ridge above. When you cross a track, descend the hillside on the same path. Chipude lies across the valley. Go over the road once more, and then cross a shallow valley.

Rejoining the road, now follow it to the right, into **Chipude**. Notice the isolated BREEZE-BLOCK

GARAGE with blue doors on your right. Just 130m beyond it, cross the road and climb the stone-laid path at the left of a house with TURNED WOODEN BALUSTRADES round a patio (FINGERPOSTS; still the **GR 131**). This takes you up through the village, to the BAR CANDELARIA, BUS STOP and CHURCH (8; **2h20min**).

Lomo del Balo, seen from the approach to Los Descansaderos

Walk 22: LA FORTALEZA

Distance: 5km/3mi; 1h55min
Grade: ● ‼ strenuous, with an overall ascent of just under 200m/650ft, but a vertiginous and potentially dangerous scramble (some climbing on all fours). You must be sure-footed and have a head for heights. Only suitable for very experienced hikers and only in fine weather. GR 131-waymarked as far as Pavon.

Equipment: walking boots, walking pole(s), sunhat, fleece, windproof, raingear, picnic, water
Access: 🚗 to/from Chipude; park opposite the church, by Bar Candelaria (28° 6.594'N, 17° 16.904'W). Or 🚌 to/from Chipude (Timetables 11, 14, 16); journey time from/to Valle Gran Rey about 1h

L a Fortaleza is everything a real mountain should be: a struggle to the top and superb views when you get there. And as you might imagine, the table-top mountain was a sacred place to the original inhabitants.

Start out at the BAR CANDELARIA in **Chipude** (**○**). Follow the main road towards San Sebastián for some 150m, then, just before BAR LA HOYA, ascend the cobbled trail to the left, the RED/WHITE-WAYMARKED **GR 131**). Cross the main road on the crest above and continue on the trail to the left of a BUS SHELTER. La Fortaleza now looms up ahead. After a minute, you reach the ROAD TO LA DAMA. Turn left and, after 50m, pick up the waymarked trail again. Cross another crest and join a village street in **El Apartadero**. Turn left and walk 250m, rejoining the main road just before BAR CAMIONEROS (**❶**). Descend the narrow trail opposite the bar into the valley below, clad in prickly pear.
Rejoining the road (**2h40min**), turn left. After 50m, turn right to ascend a cobbled lane into the little hamlet of **Pavón** (**❷**). From the end of the lane the path, flanked by small vineyards, goes right, up the V in the hillside. About three minutes uphill, at a junction on the **Degollada de Fortaleza** (**❸**; by a beauti-

fully renovated traditional house), turn right on the signposted path to La Fortaleza (*leaving* the GR 131, which heads left towards Garajonay). Half a minute up you're on the very edge of the plunging **Barranco de Erque**.
Now for the assault. Head up the path; the scramble begins at the foot of this buttress, and soon you head up a ROCK

Walkers ascending to the summit of La Fortaleza

CREVICE (**4**). Take great care: the path is well worn, stepped in places, but very steep and awkward. This hair-raising, *potentially dangerous* stretch only lasts a couple of minutes.

Above the crevice, the rock faces fall away on either side of you. Now clamber over a narrow neck of rock towards the table-topped summit. *Taking great care not to venture too close to the edge*, circle to the right, to reach a CROSS on the SUMMIT PLATEAU of **La Fortaleza** (**5**; **3h10min**). You are greeted by a magnificent vista across the southwestern corner of the island. The TRIG POINT (**6**; 1232m/4041ft) lies a few minutes further round. The large plantation you can see on the edge of plateau, high above the sea, is La Dama. The views to the east, over the deeply-gouged Barranco de Erque, will leave you in awe.

Allow 20min to circle the table-top. Back at the ROCK CREVICE (**4**), return the same way to BAR CANDELARIA in **Chipude** (**0**;

4h15min), where the bus stops. (Or return to the Degollada de Fortaleza (**3**) and follow the GR 131 to the right for 10 minutes, with grand views over the *barranco*. Meeting the road to Erque, turn left and in 10 more minutes rise to the main road, where you can hail a bus.)

Walk 23: CRUCE DE LA ZARCITA • EL CEDRO • GARAJONAY • CHIPUDE

See map overleaf; see also photos pages 7, 90 and 123
Distance: 14.6km/9mi; 4h35min
Grade: ● fairly strenuous, especially on the 650m/2100ft ascent from El Cedro to Garajonay. Best done on a fine settled day (weather conditions in this part of the island change rapidly).
Equipment: walking boots, walking pole(s), fleece, windproof, raingear, picnic, water
Access: 🚐 to Cruce de la Zarcita (Timetable 11); journey time from Valle Gran Rey 1h25min. Return on 🚐 from Chipude (Timetables 11, 14, 16); journey time to Valle Gran Rey 1h. Or 🚗 taxi back to your

car (taxi service from Bar Sonia, opposite Bar Candelaria in Chipude).
Short walk: Garajonay summit from Alto del Contadero
(2.5km/1.5mi; 40min).
● Moderate, with an ascent/descent of 250m/800ft. Stout shoes or trainers will suffice. Access by 🚗: roadside parking area at Alto del Contadero (28° 6.948'N, 17° 14.593'W), where the beautiful stone-laid Garajonay forestry track leaves the main road (nearest 🚐 stop: Pajarito). Follow the main walk from the 2h45min-point (**⑥**) to the SUMMIT (**⑦**) and return the same way.

G arajonay, the island's highest summit (1487m/4877ft), spends much of the year veiled in cloud and mist, accounting for La Gomera's abundant water supply and providing the ideal environment for the *Laurisilva* forest. This hike begins in this cool damp forest, walking alongside and over a stream. From Garajonay, you'll have a 360° panorama across the island's wooded hub and, heading home, you'll cross farmed slopes in a quiet, rarely visited valley.

Set off from **Cruce de la Zarcita** (**○**): head along the road to El Cedro and Hermigua. Just 20m from the junction, leave the road for the second path on the right, signposted to 'REVENTON OSCURO' and 'EL CEDRO'. It gives you fine views back to Los Roques. Meeting the road again after 20 minutes, cross straight over on a crazy-paved road signposted 'CASERIO DE EL CEDRO'. After 20 minutes, as the road describes a hairpin bend to the left (**40min**), you'll see two-three paths forking off to the right. Descend the path furthest to the left here. Five minutes downhill, the path leads into a large parking area behind the AULA DE LA NATURALEZA

(**①**). Descend the steps into the grounds, then turn right to pick up the path. Stay to the right of the buildings, then follow a steep path alongside a fence. This takes you back to the road, which you follow downhill. A few minutes later, just above the valley floor, a view unfolds across to El Cedro, set on a hillside of terraced gardens. This small pocket of cultivation is virtually swallowed up by the encircling hills wooded in *Laurisilva*.
You reach a junction (**55min**). *(Walk 24 joins here.)* Turn left and, at the next junction, turn left again (signposted to 'LAS MIMBRERAS'; **②**). Some three-four minutes later, take the first

Los Aceviños; roadside tapestry of houseleeks; Boca del Chorro waterfall at El Cedro (passed on Walk 39)

left turn, climbing a wide stone-laid path with steps. Ascending the valley wall, you pass several side paths; keep to the widest and clearest all the way, passing some houses. On reaching the 'PARQUE NACIONAL GARAJONAY' sign (**3**), you enter the national park. A shady path with tall spindly trees coated in moss leads you up to the small rustic chapel shown on page 90, **Nuestra Señora de Lourdes** (**4**; **1h20min**).

Beyond the picnic area and chapel, a small wooden bridge takes you over the stream and deeper into the forest. Cross another bridge and climb to a forestry track. Turn right and, after some 50m, at **Las Mimbreras** (**5**) turn left on a path signposted 'EL CONTA-DERO/ALTO DE GARAJONAY'. After five minutes the way forks. Keep left and, when the fork to the right rejoins your path ten minutes further uphill (after crossing the river bed twice), keep left again. Climbing steadily, you come to a small viewpoint looking out to Roque de Agando and El Teide on Tenerife. As you rise higher, tree heather is the dominant vegetation.

Finally you emerge on the Laguna Grande road at **Alto del Contadero** (**6**; **2h45min**). (*The Short walk begins here.*) Cross the road and head up the beautiful stone-laid forestry track opposite (sign: 'ALTO DE GARAJONAY'). Remain on this track all the way to the top. Weather permitting, you will enjoy a splendid view from the **Garajonay SUMMIT** (**7**; **3h05min**) over the undulating hills of the plateau. Chipude can be seen to the west.

Descending to Los Manantiales, and the cumbre swallowed up by cloud

Leaving the mountain, go down to the track behind the summit viewpoint (keeping right at a fork almost at once) and descend for five minutes on the pretty track you came up on. Then turn left at a junction (sign: 'CHIPUDE'). A couple of minutes later go half-right on another stone-laid track. A steep descent follows, during which you ignore a track to the left. Eventually you encounter two junctions in close succession. Go left at the first (next to a small pine wood; **3h35min**) but, at the second, take a path entering the scrub *between* the right and left forks. This becomes a track and forks after two minutes; turn right here, downhill (sign: 'CHIPUDE').

Remain on this old trail — washed out in places and overgrown with a profusion of wild flowers in spring. The descent is through a valley patched in vineyards. Rounding the hillside, drop down to the hamlet of **Los Manantiales** (❽; **4h10min**) and cross a road. Follow the trail to the right. Just past the first building, follow the path sharp left. Stepping down to a crossing path, turn left and, 50m further on (below a house), descend the second path on the right. This steep cobbled trail crosses the *barranco*. On the far side the path gently rises along the hillside up to the ridge. Round the valley above vineyards and when you reach the first houses, turn right on a cobbled lane. Follow this down to the main road in **Chipude** (❾; **4h35min**), by the CHURCH PLAZA, BAR LA CANDELARIA and BUS STOP.

Walk 24: EL CEDRO CIRCUIT FROM LAS MIMBRERAS

See also photographs on pages 87, 88 amd 123

Distance: 6km/3.5mi; 1h45min

Grade: ● Mostly easy, but with a steep and slippery 15min descent to El Cedro. Over-all ascents/descents of 200m/650ft. You must be sure-footed

Equipment: walking boots, walking pole(s), fleece, wind-proof, raingear, picnic, water; *torch for the tunnel (optional)*

Access: 🚌 to Las Mimbreras (28° 7.460'N, 17° 13.402'W). To get there, turn down the El Cedro road at Reventón Oscuro and take the first left turn (after 1.5km): this forestry track is signposted 'Arroyo de El Cedro'. The Las Mimbreras parking area is 1.8km further on.

NB: Where the two routes overlap, waypoint numbers correspond to those for Walk 24.

D on't be surprised if you're completely enveloped by mist on this walk — an ideal way to cool down on a hot day. Swathes of lichen hanging from the trees testify to the moisture in the air here. El Cedro has double the average annual precipitation for the island and four times that of coastal areas! So it is one of the island's chief places to collect water — and you can see a 'water tunnel' … if you've brought a good torch.

Start out at **Las Mimbreras** (❺) by continuing along the track signposted towards LOS ACEVIÑOS. (*Mimbreras,* by the way — Spanish for willows —

contain salicylic acid, and like all other willows were used as analgesics). The track climbs gently before levelling out after about 20 minutes, affording

Nuestra Señora de Lourdes

glimpses through the lichen-festooned trees towards Hermigua, the Barranco del Cedro and the sea.

Eventually you can turn sharp right on a path signposted 'CASERIO EL CEDRO' (❶; **40min**). Just 40m downhill, at a Y-fork, turn right on another path and a minute later turn right again. Zigzag steadily downhill for about 15 minutes, to a TARRED LANE. Go straight across, then bear right on a skiddy path to descend a ridge between terraces. At the bottom, join the road, cross the car park and head into restaurant LA VISTA at **El Cedro**.

After perhaps taking a break, descend steps from the restaurant terrace down to a paved trail. Turn right along this trail, below the camping area. In two minutes, as you approach the stream, you might like to peek into the WATER TUNNEL a few metres to the left. If you venture into it at all, be sure to use a strong torch; it's pitch black and 550m long. The tunnel emerges near a hairpin bend (with parking space) on the road between Reventón Oscuro and the GM1. If you don't suffer from claustrophobia, you can make a circuit via the tunnel (see the map for Walk 39 on page 121).

Past the tunnel entrance, ford the stream and turn left up a road (**1h10min**). Then turn right at the first junction for 'LAS MIMBRERAS' (❷). After the second house on the left, turn left, climbing a wide stone-laid PATH WITH STEPS. Ascending the valley wall, you pass several side paths; keep to the widest and clearest all the way, passing some houses and coming to a sign at the boundary of the National Park ('PARQUE NACIONAL GARAJONAY'; ❸).

A shady path with tall spindly moss-coated laurels leads you steadily up to a small rustic chapel, **Nuestra Señora de Lourdes** (❹; **1h35min**), with picnic tables, benches and a piped spring (coming out of a tree!). Beyond the chapel, a small wooden bridge takes you over the stream and deeper into the forest. Cross another bridge and climb back to the forestry track where you parked. Turn right and, after some 50m, you're back at **Las Mimbreras** (❺; **1h45min**).

Walk 25: FROM TARGA TO PLAYA DE SANTIAGO

Distance: 8km/5mi; 2h20min
Grade: ● easy descent of 700m/2300ft on a clearly defined track
Equipment: stout shoes or trainers, sunhat, fleece, raingear, picnic, plenty of water

Access: 🚐 to the Targa turn-off on the road to Alajeró (Timetables 13, 16); journey time from Playa de Santiago 15min. Return by 🚐 (Timetables 13, 17) or ⛴ (Timetable 18) from Playa de Santiago

This lazy-day ramble descends the ridge between the Barranco de la Junta and the Barranco de Santiago on a meandering track down grassy slopes. For the very fit, it could be combined with the well-signposted GR 132 to make an energetic circuit from Santiago via Antoncojo.

Start out at the *TARGA TURN-OFF* on the road to Alajeró (**○**). Walk along past colourful garden plots to the village of **Targa** (**❶**) and keep right, below the main part of the village, when the road forks. After 150m you have a choice of routes: you can stay on the road, or turn right on the path signposted *'ANTONCOJO, PLAYA DE SANTIAGO POR GR 132'* (**❷**). If you turn right here, be sure to keep left when the GR path forks right for Antoncojo; you will pass a GR 132 100KM

marker on the left after about 50m and rejoin the route I prefer at (**❸**).
I like to continue along the road, just making for the tall communication mast ahead. In 10 minutes the road will take you to a spectacular *VIEWPOINT* over Santiago and the airport. These views stay with you as the road reverts to a washed-out track high above the **Barranco de Santiago**.
You pass the *MAST* (**❹**) and, some 600m further on, the path

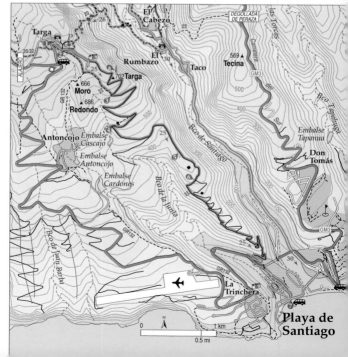

From a waterside café in Playa de Santiago

route comes in from the right (**③**). After 35 minutes on the track, you cross old paths (**④**) to an ABANDONED HOMESTEAD on the right and a SMALL RESERVOIR on the left. In the distance you can see the houses of Antoncojo. Further down another landmark is a WATER TANK (**⑤**), probably empty. When the zigzagging ends and the track straightens out, you pass a GATED ENTRANCE (**⑥**) to another abandoned property. Beyond some electricity poles and another abandoned house below you, the track fades somewhat: it veers right, towards the **Barranco de la Junta**.

A few minutes before reaching the main road, the track becomes a tarred lane. Three minutes later, you meet the main road and turn left. Just 100m further on, keep right into **Playa de Santiago** (**⑦**; **2h20min**).

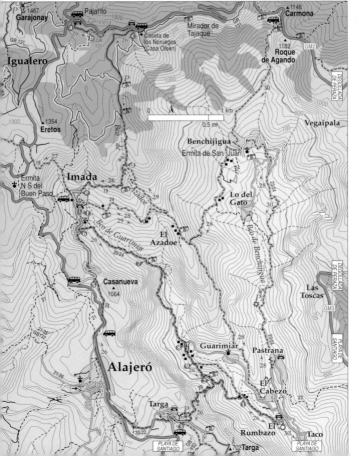

Walk 26: BARRANCO DE GUARIMIAR CIRCUIT

See map opposite; see also photos pages 8, 28 and 99
Distance: 11.7km/7.3mi; 4h30min
Grade: ●❗ very strenuous, with overall ascents/descents of about 900m/2950ft. You must be sure-footed, with a head for heights. Don't attempt in wet or windy weather. Well signposted trails.
Equipment: walking boots, walking pole(s), fleece, wind-proof, sunhat, raingear, picnic, water
Access: 🚗 to/from a lay-by with walkers' signboard at the El Rumbazo turn-off (28° 3.578'N, 17° 12.812'W). Nearest 🚌 access is the Targa turn-off (see Walk 25 and join the circuit at Targa)

Alternative walk: Barranco de Guarimiar from Pajarito (9km/5.6mi; 3h20min). ●❗ Moderate linear route, with a descent of about 1350m/4400ft. Some gravelly, slippery paths, otherwise grade and equipment as main walk. Access: 🚌 from San Sebastián to the Pajarito junction (Timetable 11); journey time about 35min. Return by pre-arranged 🚗 taxi from the El Rumbazo turn-off (allow plenty of time to finish the hike). Or walk from there down to Playa de Santiago (4km/2.5mi; 1h) to catch a bus or boat.

Start out at **Pajarito** (**ⓐ**): from the car park on the southeast side of the roundabout follow the track signposted 'LOS ROQUES'. In 4min fork left up a path (**ⓑ**; the **GR 131**). This trail rises to the main road at a wide, signposted junction (**20min**). Turn sharp right here on the forestry track signed for 'IMADA'. (The GR continues ahead, after just 50m passing a tiny concrete hut with antennas (**ⓒ**) that has given this area its local name — the *CASETA DE LOS NORUEGOS* or *CASA OLSEN*.)

Your track descends through sadly burnt laurel woods: the devastating fires of 2012 started just in this area. Slowly regener-ating, the slopes are reverting to heather, with splashes of pines and eucalyptus. The massive **Barranco de Benchijigua**, plunging away on the left, attracts your attention, while the monolithic Roque de Agando bulges up out of the landscape on the far side of the *barranco*.

Where the track swings right, you reach a small *PARKING BAY/ VIEWPOINT* (**50min**) overlooking Benchijigua far below. From here take the trail straight ahead. Overgrown vineyards lie almost unnoticed on the rock-rose- and broom-clad valley walls. A good 15 minutes down, ignore the left fork to Azadoe (**ⓓ**), cross the **Barranco de Azadoe** above a small seasonal cascade, and then keep right for Imada. The path now runs along the edge of a vertical escarpment, where you'll need a head for heights. Round-ing the nose of the ridge, you look straight down onto Imada, a biggish farming village shelter-ing high in the Barranco de Guarimiar. Looking down the *barranco*, you can trace the con-tinuation of your route below the village. Descending to a road at the upper end of **Imada** (**ⓔ**; **1h20min**), continue downhill past *BAR-CAFÉ ARCILIA* (base for Walk 27). After 350m, just past the walled-in *SPORTS GROUND* (**ⓕ**) on the left, descend steps to a lower road and continue in the same direction, passing a *CHAPEL* below left. Some 200m further on, watch for a fingerpost on the left, 'EL RUMBAZO, PLAYA DE SANTIAGO'. You have joined the main walk at (**ⓖ**); pick up the notes overleaf just past the 2h40min-point.

93

The Barranco de Guarimiar is one of the top walks on Gomera. In the depths of this sheer-sided *barranco*, a great cliff-hanging but well secured path will leave you in awe. And the path up to Targa is one of the most impressive in the Canaries, still in immaculate condition. I like to start the walk at El Rumbazo to do my climbing early on, but you could start at Targa, Alajeró or Imada. Those travelling by bus, or who just prefer to avoid *all* the climbing, can do the linear Alternative walk from Pajarito and descend into the *barranco* from the island's wooded heights — and even continue down to Playa de Santiago.

Start out from the PARKING BAY WITH WALKERS' SIGNBOARD (**O**) at the turn-off to **El Rumbazo**. Climb the steep road to the hamlet and, at the end of the road, turn sharp right up a trail passing in front of the houses. You look out across the **Barranco de Guarimiar**, teeming with palms. The village set along a hillside shelf over on the right, in the Barranco de Benchijigua, is Pastrana. The prominent finger of rock at the far end of the *barranco* is Roque de Agando, and the hamlet set on the ridge separating the two valleys is El Cabezo. After a couple of minutes ignore the fork down to a house. Crags of all shapes and sizes rise out of the valley walls above. Gardens burgeoning with produce line the valley floor, although much of the hillside terracing is abandoned. When you reach a junction by a couple of STONE BUILDINGS (**❶**; **15min**), turn left (the way ahead continues to Imada). As you climb, looking straight up towards towering overhead cliffs, you'll wonder where on earth your cobbled path goes. On reaching a sign-posted JUNCTION (**❷**; **55min**), turn left; you will return on the path to the right.

From here the path is vertiginous in places, although amply wide. You cross a *canal* spectacularly engineered in the sheer valley walls. The path winds up from ledge to ledge, clinging to jutting pieces of cliff, with a breathtaking outlook.

Crossing a PASS, you suddenly re-enter civilisation: the pretty little village of **Targa** lies before you when you meet a road (**❸**; **1h25min**). Follow the road to the right for 300m; then, just past the bend, turn right up a signposted trail ('ALAJERÓ'). In a little over 10 minutes this joins a narrow road. Go left for 75m, then pick up the trail again on the right, now wide and cobbled. Go right at the T-junction, past a

The beautifully engineered path up to Targa climbs precipitous valley walls, leaving you in awe — at times the path seems to hang in mid air.

In the Barranco de Guarimiar, not far above El Rumbazo. Guarimiar is the hamlet in the background.

threshing floor on the right. On the left is the Calvario, with the island of El Hierro in the background. When the trail meets the busy main road in **Alajeró** (**1h45min**), follow it to the right, past a BUS STOP. Keep to this road for a little over 1km (15 minutes), passing the BUS STATION up to the right. Then, just as the road curves left, go right up a trail with a FINGER-POST FOR TRAIL 20 (❹). In a good 10 minutes you meet the IMADA ACCESS ROAD (❺) on the ridge. Head right, cutting off the hairpin bends on narrow paths/steps where there's a break in the roadside barrier. Meeting the access road for the third time, follow it downhill for 200m, to the next break in the barrier. This path leads to a narrower road in the lower village of **Imada**, by FINGERPOSTS and a BREEZE-BLOCK GARAGE on the left (**2h40min**). Follow this downhill, curving left. Then, where the road bends right below a large white building, go right down concrete steps (❻; FINGER-POST FOR 'EL RUMBAZO/PLAYA DE SANTIAGO').

The path descends a bouldery slope in the **Barranco de Guarimiar**. Terracing covers the slopes all the way up to the rocky crags that line this valley. By the time the *barranco* has folded into a narrow passageway of rock, you reach a rock balcony VIEWPOINT (❼; **3h10min**). A hamlet lies far below, in a valley liberally sprinkled with palms. From the end of this rocky ledge keep down to the right, to descend the sheer nose of the ridge below you. The path seems to disappear off the end of the ridge, but in fact is built into its side. Stepping down, and very close to the edge, you discover the onward path — a narrow ledge hanging out high above the valley floor, well protected with a handrail. No need to worry about turn-offs on this stretch! Heart-beat back to normal, you cross a wide *canal* built into the valley wall (**3h30min**).

Some 20 minutes later you come to some houses in the lush and verdant lower part of **Guarimiar** (❽; **3h50min**). Before the first house, a trail heads left to the road. Ignore this; keep straight ahead, at the left of the first house. Continue along the right-hand side of the *barranco*. Five minutes or so later, keep right at a fork (❾; TRAIL 20/'TARGA'). At the next junction, you rejoin your OUTGOING ROUTE (❷; **4h10min**), soon passing a hillside buttress with a fantastic view down over the valley. Under 10 minutes later, you walk above the first house of **El Rumbazo**. The rest of them, a tight cluster, perch on the hillside. Join the road and descend to the PARKING BAY (❍; **4h30min**), where you set out.

Walk 27: GARAJONAY CIRCUIT FROM IMADA

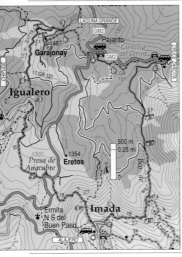

See photograph page 28
Distance: 10.4km/6.5mi; 3h50min
Grade: ●: moderate, with an ascent/descent of 600m/1970ft. You must be sure-footed; there is one slightly vertiginous stretch. Don't attempt in wet or windy weather. Well signposted trails.
Equipment: walking boots, walking pole(s), fleece, windproof, sunhat, raingear, picnic, water
Access: 🚌 or 🚐 (Timetable 13) to/from the Bar-Café Arcilia at the top end of Imada. Best parking is 50m along the road to the right, just before the bus stop (28° 5.151'N, 17° 14.468'W).

Here's another approach to Garajonay for those wanting something more ambitious than Short walk 23. All the climbing is done at the start of the hike, so you can relax on the homeward stretch.

Start out at BAR-CAFÉ ARCILIA (○) in **Imada**. Walk up the road for 50m, then turn left up a wide stone-laid trail with a fingerpost for 'TRAIL 19/PAJARITO'. You cross a canal (❶) in 15 minutes and have a good view over the Barranco de Guarimiar 15 minutes later. You reach the TOP OF THE RIDGE (**40min**), pass an isolated house on the right, and join the Pajarito–Alajeró road. Follow the road to the left for 30m, then walk downhill (right) to a reservoir, the **Presa de Acanabre** (❷). Skirt it to the left, beside the fence; past the outflow your trail heads up north — to a rise from where you can see Igualero.
Joining a track, continue in the same direction, then leave it in the left-hand bend, rejoining the trail. A splash of asphalt precedes your arrival at the main road in **Igualero** (❸; **1h25min**). At this point you join the **GR 131**

and follow it across the road, between a WATERHOUSE on the left and a BUS SHELTER on the right. Climb across fire-ravaged hillsides (now regenerating) for 10 minutes to a FORESTRY TRACK (❹). Turn left, then ignore tracks merging from the left after 100m, then 900m. But at a T-JUNCTION (❺) with a cobbled track, go right for just 20m. Then climb a path on the left up to a SADDLE (❻) and from there head right to the **Garajonay** SUMMIT (❼; **2h10min**), with its panoramic views.
Return to the saddle, then keep straight ahead uphill. In three minutes, at a fork, take the steep trail down right to **Pajarito**. From there descend as for Alternative walk 26 (partly through fire-damaged hillsides): follow the notes on page 93 from (ⓐ) to just past (ⓒ), where you will come back to BAR-CAFÉ ARCILIA (○; **3h50min**).

96

Walk 28: BARRANCO DE BENCHIJIGUA CIRCUIT

See also photos on pages 8, 95, 102

Distance: 11.2km/7mi; 4h20min

Grade: ● ⁝⁝ strenuous; ascents/descents of 650m/2130ft. You must be sure-footed and have a head for heights, especially for the narrow, slippery, vertiginous path between El Azadoe pass and the hamlet of El Cabezo. Don't attempt in bad weather. Well signposted trails

Equipment: walking boots, walking pole(s), sunhat, fleece, windproof, raingear, picnic, plenty of water

Access: 🚐 to/from a lay-by with walkers' signboard at the El Rumbazo turn-off (28° 3.578'N, 17° 12.812'W). No 🚌 access; see Alternative walk.

Alternative walk: From El Rumbazo to Imada via Benchijigua (9.7km/6mi; 3h35min). ● ⁝
Very strenuous, with an overall ascent of 750m/2460ft. You

must be sure-footed and have a head for heights. Don't attempt in bad weather. Well signposted trails. Equipment and access as main walk (🚐 start by taxi). Return on 🚌 from Imada (Timetable 13); journey time to Playa de Santiago 25min

Follow the main walk all the way to **El Azadoe** pass (**8**). From here you can see Imada — the village a couple of valleys away. Walk down the trail to the right. At a signposted junction a few minutes from El Azadoe, ignore the right turn for Pajarito (**a**); keep straight on. Cross the stream bed, then scramble up a rocky slope to the left. Rounding a ridge, you pass above another small hillside outpost and enter the upper reaches of the **Barranco de Guarimiar** (Walk 26), another tributary of the Barranco de Santiago. The valley narrows to a shady passageway, dropping in leaps

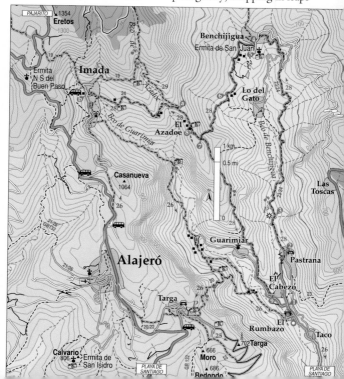

and bounds. Passing a lone house, descend into the terraced gardens of Imada, embellished with palms. The trail — by now a beautiful cobbled path — rises to the upper road in **Imada** (**Ⓑ**; **3h35min**), opposite the BAR-CAFÉ ARCILIA, base for Walk 27, an ideal refuelling stop. Your BUS STOP is just opposite the bar.

The Barranco de Benchijigua, below the imposing mass of Roque de Agando, is a patchwork quilt of terracing dotted with palms. Its hidden hamlets disclose thick-walled homesteads built in traditional style.

Start out from the PARKING BAY WITH WALKERS' SIGNBOARD (**Ⓞ**) at the turn-off to **El Rumbazo**. Continue up the valley at the right of the stream bed and go right at the Y-fork after 150m (**❶**; you will return from the left). At the end of the road, just before the ELECTRICITY SUB-STATION, climb a path up to the picturesque village of **Pastrana** (**❷**) and turn left on the village road. When this road ends, follow the wide path straight ahead, at the left of the turning point (FINGERPOST: 'ROQUE DE AGANDO').

You pass a few houses and sheds; then, ignoring minor turn-offs, descend into the **Barranco de Benchijigua**. Soon, looking over the stream bed, an enormous bulging pillar of rock high in the V of the *barranco* captures your attention — Roque de Agando. The trail follows either the stream bed or a small path on the left of the bed. After 100m you pass a small *molino de gofio** on the left (**❸**). At first glance it looks like a just another small abandoned house, but it is a mill where maize is ground and roasted. About 100m further on, the trail rises to the right, crosses a water pipe and climbs above two WATER TANKS. The ravine gives one final twist, then straightens out to reveal the village of Lo del Gato, set on a terraced hillside adorned with palms. Grassy inclines and a loose scattering of pines give the surrounding hills an alpine aspect.

Where a path forks left to Lo del Gato (**40min**), keep right, continuing straight on around the hillside on a path that is very washed out in places. You cross a watercourse and come to the Lo del Gato road (**1h15min**), where you turn left. After 140m, rejoin your path on the right, ascending the hillside. Eucalyptus and mimosas welcome you into **Benchijigua** (**❹**). At a T-junction immersed in prickly pear, turn right. You pass below some remnants of the village and some charming renovated cottages. Cross a bouldery stream bed and come to a crest with a motorable track, where the **Ermita de San Juan** sits up to the left (**❺**; **1h30min**). The rocky crest here commands a magnificent view over the village, and indeed the whole valley.

From the *ermita* walk back under 100m, then turn left and continue past a long building with a 'BENCHIJIGUA' NAME-PLATE: follow the farm track

---

*Gofio is a popular local food. It's made into a thick paste and mixed with stews and soups or with honey, bananas, almonds, even cheese. The savouries are an acquired taste; the sweets are addictive! Freshly-ground *gofio* is very aromatic.

descending behind the chained barrier, signposted for 'IMADA'. Some derelict buildings stand above, with houseleeks and *verode* growing out of their roof tiles. Somewhat over 100m downhill, ignore a fork to the left. Five minutes later, pass above some derelict houses. Opposite the last house, where the track descends, turn right on a level path. In early spring the hillsides here are splashed with pink almond blossom. Below you is a small RESERVOIR. Some 20 minutes from Benchijigua, you cross a crest above some DERELICT FARM BUILDINGS (**6**). From here the route scales the steep valley wall ahead in tight zigzags, keeping near the narrow strip of almond trees on the left-hand side of the escarpment. Continue on the gravelly path around the hillside, then ascend to an overgrown ALMOND ORCHARD and the grassy slopes beyond it. On coming to a T-JUNCTION (**7**) near the top, turn right. Ascend

to **El Azadoe Pass** (**8**; **2h40min**), from where you look back over the Benchijigua Valley, an immense bowl scooped out of the *cumbre*. Over the pass lies a quite different landscape, where greenery is woven into the sheer valley walls. This valley drops down into another, deeper and darker valley, the Barranco de Guarimiar (Walk 26). Just below you sit the remains of the hamlet of **El Azadoe**, buried in prickly pear.

Enjoy the view, then return to the JUNCTION just below the pass (**7**). Now keep straight ahead (the right-hand fork, cairned). Ignore all descending paths. At a faint fork above **Guarimiar** (**3h25min**), turn left for EL CABEZO. The path may be a little overgrown, so keep an eye out for the cairns. When you reach **El Cabezo** (**9**), descend to a road and turn right. At the next junction turn left. Follow this road down to the PARKING BAY at **El Rumbazo** (**O**; **4h**)

El Cabezo, caught by a ray of sunlight at the end of the day

Walk 29: BARRANCO DE AZADOE CIRCUIT

Nearby photos pages 8, 28, 102
Distance: 4km/2.5mi; 1h30min
Grade: ●: moderate, with ascents/descents of 250m/820ft.

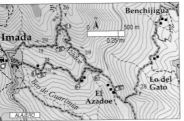

You must be sure-footed and have a head for heights. Don't attempt in bad weather. Well signposted trails
Equipment: walking boots, walking pole(s), sunhat, fleece, windproof, raingear, picnic, water
Access: 🚗 or 🚌 (Timetable 13) to/from the Bar-Café Arcilia at the top end of Imada. Best parking is 50m along the road to the right, just before the bus stop (28° 5.151'N, 17° 14.468'W).

Short and sweet. This is an ideal leg-stretcher during Car tour 5, when you wouldn't have time for the 'big' *barranco* walks in this area. You sample small bits of both Walk 28 (outgoing) and Walk 26 (on the return), linked by a stretch above the Barranco de Azadoe.

Start out CAFÉ ARCILIA (○) in Imada: take the road to the right of the BUS STOP (finger-post: 'TRAIL 24, BENCHIJIGUA'), passing the small car park on your right. When the road ends keep ahead on a paved path, descending through a myriad of healthy terraces. Keep to this paved path, crossing a stream bed. When the path veers right to some houses, continue straight ahead up a sometimes stepped trail. You pass a LONE HOUSE (❶; **10min**) from where there are fine views down the Barranco de Guarimiar and Santiago to the coast. The trail then rounds the nose of a ridge, passing a small HILLSIDE OUTPOST (❷; **20min**), from where the Barranco de Azadoe is visible. Continue downhill, cross a stream bed and then rise up to a Y-fork (❸; **30min**). Bear left here, following the sign for 'PAJARITO'.*
The trail rises and immediately

swings hard left in front of two RUINS, initially running above your outward route, then levelling out and delving deeper into the **Barranco de Azadoe**, where the major climb begins, some of it paved. There is so much vegetation to intrigue the eye that the ascent is softened, especially when the trail zigzags away from the stream bed from time to time. With terraces left, right and ahead, you come back to the *barranco* above a small seasonal cascade, joining the route of Alternative walk 26, which comes in from Pajarito (❹; **1h05min**).
Turn left here, crossing the stream bed, and then keep right for Imada. From now on it's all downhill, *but* first: the path now runs along the edge of a vertical escarpment, where you'll need a head for heights. Rounding the nose of the ridge, you look straight down onto Imada, high in the Barranco de Guarimiar. Descending to a road at the upper end of the village, continue downhill, back to BAR-CAFÉ ARCILIA and the BUS STOP (○; **1h30min**).

*If you were to continue straight on you would come in a few minutes to El Azadoe, a major junction on Walk 28.

Walk 30: BARRANCO DE SANTIAGO

More photos pages 92, 99
Distance: 12km/7.4mi; 3h40min
Grade: ● ： fairly easy descent of
1100m/3600ft. But the first half
hour is steep, and pine needles
underfoot make it slippery. You
must be sure-footed and have a
head for heights on a couple of
short stretches. Don't attempt in
wet weather. Good signposting
Equipment: walking boots,
walking pole(s), sunhat, fleece,
windproof, raingear, picnic,
plenty of water
Access: 🚐 to Roque de
Agando (Timetable 11); journey
time from San Sebastián 35min.
Return on 🚐 from Playa de
Santiago (Timetable 13)
**Shorter walk: From Roque de
Agando to Pastrana** (6.5km/
4mi; 2h30min). ● Grade as
main walk, but the descent is just
800m/2600ft. Equipment and
access as main walk. Return by
🚕 pre-arranged taxi from
Pastrana (or telephone for a taxi
on arrival: 34 922 895022).

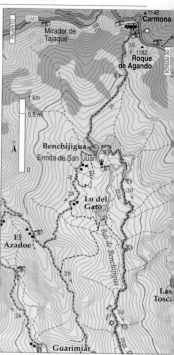

The Barranco de Santiago is not one of those 'love at
first sight' ravines. But once beyond its stark and
inhospitable façade, the most unexpected sight greets you
— a boulder-strewn floor crammed with gardens and
orchards. Small hamlets and pretty palms decorate the
valley walls, while in winter a stream adds to the beauty.
Deeper in among the hills, weird and wonderful rocks —
none moreso than Agando — burst out of the landscape.

From the FOREST FIRE MEMORIAL
(◎) at the foot of **Roque de
Agando** take the cobbled trail
signposted to '*BENCHIJIGUA*'
(*TRAIL 23*). After passing below
the foot of Roque de Agando,
you cross a covered *canal* (❶)
and then the stony bed of the
Barranco de Benchijigua
(**30min**).
When you reach **Benchijigua** —
just a few houses, some burnt-
out, others lived in (❷; **1h
05min**), be sure to take a break

at the **Ermita de San Juan**, to
enjoy the view shown overleaf.
Returning from the *ermita*, turn
right along the motorable track,
but after 50m turn right down
the green/white waymarked trail
for '*PASTRANA*' (❸) — briefly
descending a *barranco* bed and
passing below some beflowered
cottages. Cross another small
barranco and ascend to a low
crest. Turn left and descend to
the LO DEL GATO ROAD below
(**1h20min**). Follow this road

101

View north to Roque de Agando, from near the Ermita de San Juan in Benchijigua (1h30min)

left uphill for about 150m, then pick up your ongoing trail on the right (**4**). After about 20 minutes ignore the trail off right to Lo del Gato (**5**). In another 20 minutes you pass two WATER TANKS, then drop into the stream bed and find an old, but still functional, *GOFIO MILL* on the right (**6**; see footnote on page 98).

The trail climbs up left from the stream bed and rises to **Pastrana** (**7**; **2h30min**) and the end of a road coming from Playa de Santiago. Follow the road for 120m, then turn right (FINGER-POST: 'EL RUMBAZO/PLAYA DE SANTIAGO'; **8**). This path drops you down to a lower road beside the **Barranco de Santiago**, which you follow via **Taco** for just over 5km down to **Playa de Santiago** (**9**; **3h40min**).

Walk 31: DEGOLLADA DE PERAZA CIRCUIT VIA LA LAJA AND ROQUE DE AGANDO

See map overleaf; see also photos pages 25 and 26
Distance: 8.2km/5mi; 3h15min
Grade: ● ? strenuous, with an initial descent of 400m/1300ft, followed by an ascent of 600m/1970ft. You must be sure-footed and have a head for heights. Don't attempt in wet or windy weather. Good trails
Equipment: walking boots, walking pole(s), sunhat, fleece,

windproof, raingear, picnic, plenty of water
Access: ⛟ or 🚐 to/from the Degollada de Peraza (Timetables 11, 13, 17); journey time from San Sebastián 20min, from Playa de Santiago 1h. By car park at the bar-restaurant (28° 5.916'N, 17° 10.989'W) if you plan to eat there; otherwise park by the Ermita de la Nieves (28° 6.062'N, 17° 12.117'W) and start there.

The Barranco de Las Lajas, the setting for this walk, is a picturesque valley with a number of reservoirs and, higher up, cascading streams and pine-wooded slopes. This classic hike makes a short steep descent down towards the rustic village of La Laja, followed by a short steep climb back up to the crest, from where you overlook a number of curiously-shaped volcanic chimneys — Los Roques.

The walk starts at the **Mirador de La Laja** (○). Descend the signposted path at the right of the viewpoint balcony. This superbly-cobbled path leads down the hillside to La Laja (although the village is still in hiding far down to the left). Initially you overlook a valley of tumbling ridges. Just keep to the cobbled *camino* all the way down. Crossing the first ridge, the Roques appear higher up in the valley: La Zarcita (left) and Ojila (right) — smooth conical volcanic chimneys. Thick, fleshy-leafed aloe plants proliferate on these barren inclines. Some 35 minutes down from the pass, charming La Laja comes into view (❶), a small strung-out village. Ten minutes later, from the crest of a sharp ridge, you find the ideal VIEWPOINT over this peaceful little haven (❷; **45min**).
At this viewpoint, *leave* the main path, and follow the left-hand fork along the steep hillside at the edge of the pine woods,

passing *above* the village of **La Laja**. Take care: the pine needles are very slippery underfoot. A bubbling stream and the green *barranco* bed below enhance the freshness of the valley floor. Five minutes later, the other path rejoins from the right. Continue above the village for another couple of minutes, then come to another fork.
This next fork, signposted 'ROQUE DE AGANDO' (❸; **1h**), marks the beginning of your ascent: keep left here. A steep climb through pines follows. Ignore any minor paths to the left or right. The trail crosses four stream beds on wooden bridges or planks. Higher up you reach an enchanting old ramshackle SHELTER with a veranda at the **Degollada del Tanque** (❹; CASA DEL MANCO; **1h45min**), on a crest at the edge of the wood. From here three volcanic chimneys are in view, the product of lava that solidified inside volcanic vents. On the left is Carmona, and the other two

you identified earlier in the hike. Roque de Agando rises behind the crest to the left.

To make for the main road near Roque de Agando, take the path at the left of the shelter, to continue up the spine of the ridge (don't take the path behind the shelter). On the ascent, a wonderful panorama unfolds over the faded-green valleys below. Tenerife sits in the background, clearly outlined.

Eventually you reach the main road just below and to the east of **Roque de Agando** (**5**; **2h20min**). Turn left on the road to continue the walk (or first follow the road to the *right* for a few minutes, to a forest fire memorial and *mirador*, for a fine view down into the Barranco de Benchijigua and the route of Walk 30). Some 240m along, turn left uphill with the **GR 131** (**6**; 'DEGOLLADA DE PERAZA'). After 10 minutes or so the trail descends to a track, which takes you down to the **Ermita de las Nieves** (**7**; **2h40min**). Picnic facilities have been set up here, to take advantage of the magnificent panorama.

From the chapel follow the lane downhill. After 10 minutes, 50m before the lane turns sharp right downhill to the main road, head left uphill on a track (**8**; still the **GR 131**). Another track joins from the right and you pass two masts. Don't miss the magnificent views down into the Barranco de Las Lajas from the edge of the escarpment here, but be careful if it's windy! When the track fizzles out after 10 minutes, continue on the cobbled trail, which almost at once begins to drop steeply down to the main road below, 100m west of the **Mirador de La Laja** (**9**; **3h10min**).

Casa del Manco at the Degollada del Tanque, dwarfed by Roque de Ojila (top); the trail from La Laja up to Roque de Agando (bottom)

Walk 32: CIRCUIT FROM JERDUÑE VIA SEIMA AND THE CASAS DE CONTRERA

See also photograph page 111
Distance: 11km/6.8mi; 4h10min
Grade: ●: moderate-strenuous, with a descent/ascent of 600m/1970ft. You must be sure-footed and have a head for heights. Don't attempt in wet or windy weather or on hot days *(no shade)*. All on signposted paths
Equipment: walking boots, walking pole(s), sunhat, fleece, raingear, picnic, plenty of water
Access: 🚌 to/from a layby on the east side of the GM3 (Carretera del Sur) just south of the Degollada de Peraza (28° 5.917'N, 17° 11.199'W); if there is no room, park at Bar Peraza (28° 5.914'N, 17° 10.988'W) — and give them some custom! In either case, walk south on the GM3 to the KM1 marker and head up the track to the left *(not signposted when last checked)*. This merges with a cut-off piece of the old road, where the walk begins. Or

🚌 to/from Jerduñe (Timetables 13, 17); journey time from San Sebastián 20min and walk 400m north to the KM1 marker. You could also take a 🚌 to/from the Degollada de Peraza (Timetables 11, 13, 17); journey time from San Sebastián 20min; from Playa de Santiago 1h.
Alternative walk: From Jerduñe to Playa de Santiago (14km/8.7mi; 3h35min). ●: Strenuous, with ascents of about 250m/820ft and descents of 1150m/3800ft overall; otherwise grade/access/equipment as main walk. It makes sense to leave a car in Playa de Santiago and *start* the walk by bus (as above), rather than wait for a bus back to your car. Follow the main walk to the JUNCTION at (④), then turn right on **Trail 25**. At the **Casas de Contrera** (⑥), turn right again and follow **Walk 33** from ⑥ to the end. See map on page 108.

Elevated grassy valleys and abandoned derelict farming settlements are the hallmark of this hike, and right from the outset the dramatic approach above canyon-sized valleys puts you in a hiking mood.

The walk starts at the BEND OF THE OLD CARRETERA DEL SUR (**○**) reached via a gritty track rising from KM1 on the GM3, 400m east of **Jerduñe** and 1km south of the **Degollada de Peraza**. Leave the old road in the hairpin bend by a sign, 'MONUMENTO NATURAL BARRANCO DEL CABRITO': take the path that heads towards the right-hand side of the **Tacalcuse Ridge**. The village set on the prickly pear-covered slopes over to your right is Jerduñe. Rounding the side of the ridge, you arrive at a sheltered COL (**1**), to discover the couple of buildings of **Berruga**.

Keeping to the left of the buildings, the path then returns to the west side of the ridge, where a view unfolds down into the **Barranco de los Castredores**. The wide but somewhat vertiginous path descends along the base of the craggy crest, the **Alto de Tacalcuse** (**2**; **40min**).

After a short climb onto a ridge, the Playa de Santiago's Hotel Tecina and golf course — where the Alternative walk is heading — come into view. Soon you'll spot the interesting OUTPOST (**3**) shown opposite above you, built into and around the Tacalcuse rock face. You pass below this abandoned dwelling.

Under 10 minutes later, on coming to a SIGNPOSTED JUNCTION (**4**; **1h05min**), turn left for 'SEIMA/EL CABRITO'. Later in the main walk you'll return to this junction from Casas de Contrera off to the right. *(But if you are doing the Alternative walk,*

*turn right here (due south) here, to go directly to Casas de Contrera, then pick up Walk 33 at its 4h50min-point (**6**).)*

Gentle grassy slopes littered with stone walls roll away ahead of you now, and El Teide stands out clearly on the horizon over to the left. Soon you arrive at the edge of the strikingly severe **Barranco Juan de Vera**. A few minutes later you overlook Seima, its abandoned stone dwellings scattered over a hillside of rocks and grass not far below.

After less than 10 minutes' descent, you're looking down on a derelict building with a sprawling brilliant-green pepper tree in front of it. Pass to the left of the building and to the right of the next one. During the next 10 minutes, go left at a fork and, on entering the centre of **Seima** (latterly called 'Morales', but to me it will always be Seima!; **5**; **1h35min**), turn right at a SIGN-POSTED FORK.

Follow the clear trail around the valley. Once in a while you will spot the faded red/white flashes of the **GR 132**. After clambering over a natural wall of broken rock, you see Casas de Contrera, an old farmstead two *barrancos* away. Past the first *barranco* (**Barranco de Guincho**), keep right at a fork. The trail fades as you approach the second stream bed, **Barranco de Contrera**: continue up the valley floor for about 50m, following the faint waymarks and cairns. The abandoned **Casas de Contrera** (**6**; **2h20min**) were once a thriving small community where cereal crops were grown. Some

About 15 minutes from the Alto de Tacalcuse you pass below an outpost built into the rock face; right: the Casas de Contrera — focussing on what was once a fine two-story house

artefacts are lying about, but take care; the masonry may be weak.

To return to the old road and the GM3, take *SIGNPOSTED TRAIL* 25 that ascends to the left of the main two-storied house. Climb the rocky crest behind the house. After about 15 minutes, you pass to the right of a derelict *STONE BUILDING, WITH A WHEAT THRESHING FLOOR* just below. High gentle slopes keep appearing, revealing the remains of an amazingly large area of cultivation in the past.

A little over 10 minutes above the last building, some *MORE BUILDINGS* appear at the right of the path. A couple of minutes further uphill, the trail crosses bedrock. Continue straight uphill, and ignore the minor path going off to the right. After the remains of a low wall appear to the right of the path, the trail is again clearly defined.

Back at the *SEIMA JUNCTION* (❹; **3h**), turn left to rejoin your outgoing path, quickly passing the house shown above (❸). From the pass at **Berruga** (❷) continue up to the old road and then the GM3 (**4h10min**). Return to your car or, if you've come by bus, walk on to Jerduñe or the Degollada de Peraza.

Walk 33: FROM SAN SEBASTIAN TO PLAYA DE SANTIAGO

Map begins on page 113, ends below; photos pages 92, 108
Distance: 19km/12mi; 7h
Grade: ●❗ very strenuous and long, with ascents/descents of 1100m/3600ft overall, on stony paths. You must be sure-footed and have a head for heights on the climb over to El Cabrito. Red/white waymarking throughout (GR 132). *No shade!*
Equipment: walking boots, walking pole(s), sunhat, fleece, raingear, swimwear, picnic, plenty of water

Access: 🚌 (Timetables 11, 12, 13, 17) or ⛴ (Timetable 18) to San Sebastián. Return on 🚌 (Timetable 13) or ⛴ (Timetable 18) from Playa de Santiago
Shorter walk: From San Sebastián to Playa de la Guancha and back (9km/5.6mi; 2h40min). ● Moderate, with ascents/descents of 400m/1300ft overall; access and equipment as above. Follow the main walk to **Playa de la Guancha** (**1h20min**) and return the same way.

Up at the crack of dawn, you'll catch the sun rising over the *cumbre* and perhaps see the morning ferry sailing across to Tenerife. Then, struggling in and out of *barrancos,* you'll cross a barren landscape strewn with rock, where ravines narrow into shady fissures. At the mouth of one of these sits the tiny outpost of El Cabrito — an oasis of greenery accessible only by boat or on foot.

Setting out from **San Sebastián** (◎), follow the beachside promenade southwest. Pass the FOOTBALL GROUND, then turn right and take the river bed road/track to ENDESA (the town power plant). Immediately past the plant gates, go left on the SIGNPOSTED PATH running along-

side the chain-link fence surrounding the plant's grounds (RED/WHITE WAYMARKS OF THE GR 132). After a few minutes uphill, the remains of an old cobbled path come underfoot.
A 20-minute climb brings you to the crest of a ridge. The path

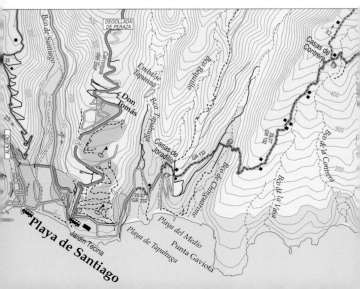

Playa del Cabrito

then passes above a WOODEN CROSS which topples over from time to time, from where there is a fine view back to the capital. On the slopes high above stands the great Sacred Heart monument. You cross the **Barranco del Revolcadero** (❶; **40min**) and, still ascending, cross the faint remains of a dirt track.

Thirty minutes later you cross another ridge (**1h10min**) and catch sight of Playa del Cabrito, set deep in the sheer coastline ahead, and Playa de la Guancha directly below, a lonely beach set in a forbidding landscape of dark

jagged cliffs rising from an aquamarine sea. The path twists down into a side-ravine and through a dry, boulder-strewn stream bed, where lime-green *balo* floods the *barranco* floor. You pass a cottage and some shacks behind **Playa de la Guancha** (❷; **1h20min**). This is a good place to swim, but *take care:* the beach shelves steeply. *The Short walk returns from this beach.*

From here the route continues past the cottage and shacks up the right-hand side of the **Barranco de la Guancha**. Some 20 minutes from the beach, the

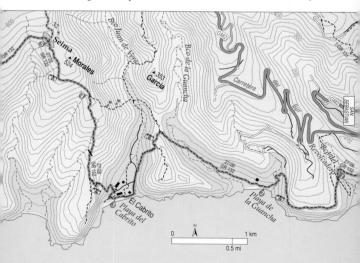

way swings left across the
barranco (**1h40min**) and climbs
the far side. Fifteen minutes up,
the path suddenly turns left, up
stone steps. (Ignore the faint
trail to the right here — it was
originally a variation of the GR,
but has not been maintained by
the *cabildo*.)
On reaching a CREST (**2h10min**),
an exhilarating sight greets you:
you look straight down into a
deep *barranco*, where knurls
(knobby ridges resembling steep
stairways) tumble down the
sides. To the left you spot the
corner of a tiny Garden of Eden
— El Cabrito. The full beauty of
this verdant outpost is revealed a
little further on, when you look
down on its tapestry of banana
groves, fruit trees and vegetable
plots. To reach it, head up left,
then cross over to the right-hand
side of this sheer ridge, where a
steep, gravelly path drops you in
zigzags down into the **Barranco
Juan de Vera**.
The **El Cabrito** *finca* (formerly a
croft, now a holiday resort for
those who want to get
away from it all) sits behind the
thick stone wall that keeps the
barranco from overflowing after
heavy rain. Cross the *barranco*
and follow the wall to the left for
some 100m, then use the stone
'steps' to climb over the wall
(FINGERPOST) and turn left along
a track to the long and pebbly
Playa del Cabrito (**③**; **2h
35min**). Continue along the
shore. It should be possible to
get some refreshments at the
picnic area near the southern end
of the beach, to sustain you for
the next four hours; certainly
there is water on tap beside the
restaurant. Near the quay, follow
the walkway to the right, into a
plantation. By a row of houses,
pick up your ongoing cobbled
trail to the left. (When the way

forks above some plots, turn
sharp left.)
The well-cobbled trail takes you
huffing and puffing up to a FLAT-
TOPPED CREST (**3h15min**).
Follow the crest inland and
scramble over a dyke. Higher
up, you briefly enter a watercourse and leave it on a faint trail
that curves to the left. At a
junction just below the crest (**④**;
the other end of the faint,
neglected GR variation), keep
left. Higher still (**4h**), you catch
a glimpse of the Hotel Tecina
and the gardens above Santiago
and then the abandoned hamlet
of Seima, superbly located in
open countryside overlooking
the sea. A little over five minutes
later you pass through **Seima**
(**⑤**; **4h05min**; also called
Morales). Have a look at the
well-preserved old oven *(horno)*
just below the first cluster of
buildings (on your right). Then
pass through a row of
abandoned houses until you
reach a junction, where there is
another old *horno* behind a stone
wall on the right. (*Walk 32 joins
at this junction.*)
Turn left here and follow the
clear trail around the valley.
Once in a while you will spot the
faded RED/WHITE FLASHES OF THE
GR 132. After clambering over a
natural wall of broken rock, you
see Casas de Contrera, an old
farmstead two *barrancos* away.
Past the first *barranco* (**Barranco
de Guincho**), keep right at a
fork. The trail fades as you
approach the second stream bed,
Barranco de Contrera: just
continue up the valley floor for
about 50m, following the faint
waymarks and cairns.
On reaching the abandoned
Casas de Contrera (**⑥**;
4h50min), you'll probably want
to explore the main building —
the grand two-storied house

shown on page 107. The trail forks below this house (SIGNPOST): your onward route goes down to the left. (*Walk 32 takes the trail ascending to the left of the house.*)

After five minutes, you cross a dry stream bed. Re-crossing almost at once, keep to the main trail, passing below farm buildings. A good 10 minutes from Contrera, ignore a path ascending to the left. Then pick up the main stream again (**Barranco de la Vasa**): cross it and pass THREE STONE HOUSES in succession (**5h10min**).

The trail descends beside and then in a tiny *barranco*. After crossing the *barranco*, it passes to the right of a STONE BUILDING and then bends right. Ten minutes later you reach the edge of the *barranco*. From here the route descends steadily into the meagre banana groves of the **Barranco de Chingua-rime**, where you cross the river

bed and join a track (**7**; **5h50min**).

Follow the track south just a short way, then pick up the trail on the right. Below the lowest house at **Casas del Joradillo** (**8**) the old *camino* meets a road, but just past the houses you can pick up your trail again to descend into the next *barranco*. Rejoining the road, follow it almost to its highest point, then cut back right on the trail (next to a SMALL CONCRETE BUILDING). Cross the crest and descend into another *barranco*. Cross the road once more, and continue down the path. You cross yet another *barranco* and join a road at a Y-fork. Follow the road south, uphill, ignoring the road left to Playa de Tapahuga.

Now follow the road between the Hotel Jardín Tecina and the golf course to the BUS STOP in **Playa de Santiago** — on the main road, just 50m to the left (**9**; **7h**).

Early morning in San Sebastián, seen from the Parador

Walk 34: FROM LAS CASETAS TO SAN SEBASTIAN

See also photograph page 111
Distance: 10km/6.2mi; 3h15min
Grade: ●? easy-moderate, with ascents of about 300m/1000ft and an overall descent of 700m/2300ft. You must be sure-footed and have a head for heights. Don't attempt on wet or windy days: danger of rockfall. Well signposted (Trails 31 and 32)
Equipment: walking boots, sunhat, fleece, windproof, long trousers, raingear, picnic, water, dog deterrent if dogs worry you

Access: 🚌 (Timetable 12) to 'Las Casetas' on the GM1, at the junction with the Camino Forestal de Majona just northeast of KM7; journey time from San Sebastián 15min. The bus stop is *not signposted*. *Note:* the Camino Forestal de Majona is a very narrow and dangerous road, *not recommended for motorists* — too narrow for two cars to pass, with no barriers and a danger of rockfall. Return on 🚌 (Timetables 11, 12, 13, 17) from San Sebastián.

This walk is best begun early in the morning, to appreciate the spectacular play of light and shade on the *cumbre* (see photographs). There are fascinating geological strata, herds of goats and small flocks of sheep roaming grassy slopes — and hidden corners with isolated stands of palms or rocks dripping with lichen.

Start out at the 'LAS CASETAS' (●), at the junction of the **GM1 (Carretera del Norte)** and the **Camino Forestal de Majona**, where you leave your transport. Follow the mountain road *(camino forestal)* uphill. After 80m a path off left is signposted to 'ENCHEREDA'

Looking west to Los Roques from the Mirador de los Manaderos

(Trail 31). Walk 36 descends this path; if you've already done that walk you might just like to keep to the track all the way to the Gerode Pass (if so, deduct 30min from all following time checks).

But the main walk heads sharp left up this old trail. Before long you can look down over the **Barranco de Agua Jilva** and the **Barranco de la Villa** on their way to San Sebastián. And behind you lies the *cumbre*, a backbone of forested ridges radiating seaward. The path climbs steadily towards a rock arch seen high above. Reaching the top of the ridge, the **Altos de Uteza** (**❶**; **45min**), keep right on **Trail 31** and walk beneath the ROCK ARCH seen from below. From here descend

gently to the pass of **La Gerode** (**❷**; **1h05min**) — to look down north into the enormous **Barranco de las Casas** slicing into the massif.

From the pass take the sign-posted fork to the right (left is again signed to 'Enchereda'), and at a JUNCTION (**❸**) a couple of minutes further uphill keep right again on **Trail 32**. (The route to the left, to 'Cuevas Blancas', is the difficult trail followed in Alternative walk 2 of Walk 35.) Your trail, signposted to 'SAN SEBASTIAN', makes its way across the rocky hillside beside a WATER PIPE and climbs the nose of the ridge, sometimes over bedrock. Five minutes along, you reach a craggy ROCK OUTCROP below a cave. The path sidles up against the sheer face of

A spectacular play of light and shade on the cumbre ... and hidden corners with isolated stands of palms ...

waymarked rock, turn sharp right downhill. Small CAIRNS will keep you on the trail.

You descend a winding (and potentially ankle-twisting) path into a side-ravine. Some 20 minutes down from the crest, when a PATH JOINS FROM THE LEFT (⑥), keep straight on (the right-hand fork). Cross a DYKE and later enter the **Barranco del Rincón**, a narrow dry ravine lined from top to bottom with crumbled stone walls. Circle the *barranco*, ignoring a path heading back left towards Aluce at a PASS (⑦), and soon after crossing a small road pass a couple of TELEVISION AERIALS set in the rock (**2h25min**).

You eventually join a wider road; cross over to another road and pick up your path a few metres to the right. Rejoin the road, and follow it straight ahead over a ROUNDABOUT and then past houses. A good 10 minutes later, watch for RED-TILED STEPS (⑧) descending to the right, just before house No 49. Follow this stairway, ignoring crossing streets, all the way down into **San Sebastián**, where you will emerge at the church, **Nuestra Señora de la Asunción** (⑨; **3h15min**).

the ridge, which slides down into the *barranco*. Ten minutes further along, bits of rubbish, broken glass, and — usually — dogs barking, alert you to the **Casas de Jaragán** (❹; **1h20min**), a homestead high in the rock above. Continue straight ahead — beside a white- and pink-hued 'sandwich' in the rock face.

You quickly reach another CREST on the flanks of **Jaragán** (❺; **1h25min**). Walk ahead to a SIGNPOST indicating 'SAN SEBAS-TIAN' and turn left, keeping an eye open for cairns and paint marks). After some 80m along this path, when you come to a

Walk 35: CIRCUIT TO THE CUEVAS BLANCAS

Distance: 13.6km/8.4mi; 3h05min

Grade: ● moderate, *if you use our suggested route*, with overall ascents/descents of about 500m/ 1640ft. You must be sure-footed and have a good sense of direction: at times you will have to make your way over rocky terrain without a path, but it is quite straightforward *in clear weather.* (Don't attempt this walk in poor visibility or on wet or windy days.) Partly way-marked Trails 31 and 32

Equipment: walking boots, sunhat, fleece, windproof, long trousers, raingear, picnic, water, dog deterrent if dogs worry you

Access: 🚗 park at the side of the GM1 by the Camino Forestal de Majona (just northeast of KM7, about 300m before the first tunnel when coming from San Sebastián; 28° 7.422'N, 17° 9.500'W). Or 🚌 (Timetable 12) to/from 'Las Casetas' at the same location *(not signposted).*

Alternatives

1 ● Use the Camino Forestal de Majona both outward to the Gerode Pass (**2**) *and* on the return (it's only used for the return on the description below). This will save 35min.

2 ● :: Follow signposted Trail 31 from (**3**). This is the official path to 'Cuevas Blancas', but be warned that it is *very narrow and exposed (although there are some railings), potentially dangerous in wet conditions.*

There are several ways to do this hike, which can range from moderate to *very demanding* and potentially dangerous. If you *do* decide to tackle the official route (Ruta 31), then it would be best to do so on the outward leg — it's always easier going *up* exposed paths than coming down… Whichever way you choose, the rock strata seen on this hike are among the island's most interesting geological features.

Start out by following **Walk 34** on page 113 to the JUNCTION at (**3**). Since Trail 31 is an 'official' route, presumably it will be well maintained — in fact some railings have been put in place in the last couple of years. If you are opting to tackle this *narrow and vertiginous* path, then go left

at this junction, up steps hewn into the rock.

But it's far easier and safer to follow Walk 34 all the way to the crest at the 1H25MIN-POINT (**5**). Then fork left around the hillside, heading back the way you came, but now well above the (hardly visible) **Casas de**

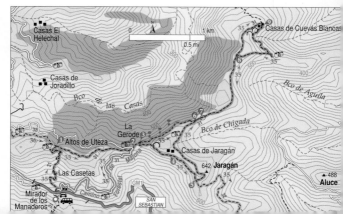

The Cuevas Blancas: built into white tuff, they are now used as storerooms.

Jaragán. Ahead you will see a GULLY WITH PALMS: descend to this gully, where you will meet the 'official' route at a JUNCTION (**6**) north of the point where it is potentially dangerous. Follow it to the right, crossing an old THRESHING FLOOR (**7**). Coming to another JUNCTION (**8**), keep to the left side of the ROCKY OUTCROP (on the return, you will rejoin your path from the right-hand fork). A little over 10 minutes later you arrive at **Casas de Cuevas Blancas** (**9**; **1h25min**). The homesteads themselves are uninhabited — and you might find an abandoned chair in a cave for your picnic lunch! From here you can see your ongoing path across the valley on your right. A rough animals' trail takes you past the 'white caves' (**Cuevas Blancas**) and onto this path.

Some 15 minutes from the homestead, as the path vanishes on a crest, follow cairns up to the ridge. Several minutes up, the way levels out, and about seven minutes later you're back on your outgoing path at (**8**): head left and retrace your outward route back to the **Camino Forestal de Majona**. Instead of retracing your steps, take this track back down to LAS CASETAS (**O**; **3h05min**).

The lone homestead of Enchereda (Walk 36) lies on the Camino Forestal de la Majona to the northwest of Las Casetas where Walks 34 and 35 begin. It almost blends in with the browns of the surrounding hills, but its bright green terraced gardens give it away.

Walk 36: FROM HERMIGUA TO LAS CASETAS VIA ENCHEREDA

See photos opposite and pages
112-13
Distance: 20km/12.4mi;
5h50min
Grade: ● strenuous, with overall ascents of 700/2300ft and a
descent of 280m/920ft. Well
signposted; partly Trail 32
Equipment: walking boots,
walking pole(s), sunhat, fleece,

windproof, long trousers, raingear, picnic, plenty of water
Access: 🚌 to Hermigua (Timetable 12); journey time from San
Sebastián 35min. Alight at the
bus stop near the DISA petrol
station, 2.8km north of the
church. Return on 🚌 from 'Las
Casetas' on the GM1 (Timetable
12); journey time 15min

Leaving the lush green banana plantations behind, you
ascend the severe walls of the Barranco de Monteforte
and bid farewell to Hermigua. Ahead lies one of the
loneliest, bleakest corners of the island. This inhospitable
landscape of razor-back ridges and sheer ravines may not
appeal to everyone. But for those who find beauty in desolate landscapes, there are heather-capped crests and a
rainbow of volcanic hues in the rock to brighten the way.

Setting out from the BUS STOP
(◉) just north of the DISA
PETROL STATION in **Hermigua**,
follow the main road south
towards San Sebastián for about
70m. Then descend the first
flight of steps on the left, dropping into the banana groves.
Cross the **Barranco de Monteforte** on a footbridge, keep
ahead for 80m, then turn right at
a T-JUNCTION with a wide lane.
At the end of the lane climb up
left to the road and turn right.
Three minutes along, fork left
uphill on a road (signposted to
'PLAYA DE LA CALETA'). Just
100m further on, at a junction,
go straight ahead, now on a lane
(FINGERPOST: 'LA CALETA'). From
here there's a good view over
Hermigua's banana plots and
beach.
Crossing the **Camiña ridge**,
turn sharp right at the junction
for 'SAN SEBASTIÁN'; (❶; **40min**),
now on a track, the **Camino
Forestal de la Meseta**. *(Walk 37
goes straight on here for 'La
Caleta'.)* An impenetrable wall
of mountains crosses the land-

scape in front of you and tumbles
off into the sea. Ascending
gradually into the hills, you find
them surprisingly green and
grassy. Trees begin appearing:
short bushy pines, palms and,
soon, junipers. The track contours, curling in and out of the
hillsides, and you join **Trail 32**
which comes down from the
right (❷). Ignore all turnings to
the left, whether signposted or
chained off and private.
Eventually you begin climbing
the **Riscos de Juel** (**2h**) in a
series of tight zigzags. You pass
through old vineyards and come
into a colony of palms. Rock
walls dripping with vegetation
rise sharply above you. Having
climbed high up the face of the
escarpment, the banana plantations of Hermigua come into
view once more. You pass a
couple of STONE FARM SHEDS
(**2h35min**) clinging to the
hillside. On cloudless days, the
view across the tumbling naked
ridges and out over the rocky
shoreline onto a white-capped
sea is superb. Further up, off a

117

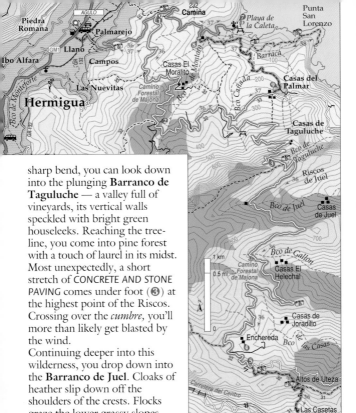

sharp bend, you can look down into the plunging **Barranco de Taguluche** — a valley full of vineyards, its vertical walls speckled with bright green houseleeks. Reaching the treeline, you come into pine forest with a touch of laurel in its midst. Most unexpectedly, a short stretch of CONCRETE AND STONE PAVING comes under foot (❸) at the highest point of the Riscos. Crossing over the *cumbre,* you'll more than likely get blasted by the wind.

Continuing deeper into this wilderness, you drop down into the **Barranco de Juel**. Cloaks of heather slip down off the shoulders of the crests. Flocks graze the lower grassy slopes, and you may bump into healthy cows and calves dawdling along the track. Later, when you enter another valley (**Barranco de Gallon**), neglected plots and the remains of stone walls tell the story of homesteads abandoned. The only sounds you'll hear are the shrill calls of the kestrel and the wing-beating of fleeing quail.

Eventually you head into yet another valley, the **Barranco de las Casas**. The homestead of **Enchereda** (❹; **4h45min**) comes into sight, almost blending in with the browns of the denuded hills. The goats are milked here at midday; the best cheese on the island reputedly comes from these hills and valleys. Along here the eroded hillsides are a feast of colour:

118

maroon, russet, faded gold, rusty orange.

Ten minutes beyond Enchereda, leave the track by climbing STEPS (❺) up to the right a minute past an ELECTRICITY SUBSTATION. A steady climb takes you up through ferns and rock-roses. You look out right over the enormous *barranco.* Twenty minutes up you come to a path junction at the **Altos de Uteza**. Turn right here and descend to the GM1 at LAS CASETAS (❻; **5h 50min**), where the Camino Forestal de Majona joins the road just east of the **Mirador de los Manaderos**. *Flag down* the bus (the stop is *not signed*).

Walk 37: EL PALMAR CIRCUIT FROM HERMIGUA

Map opposite; photo page 120
Distance: 15km/9.3mi; 4h15min
Grade: ● moderate, with over-all ascents/descents of 550m/1800ft. Well signposted; partly Trails 32 and 33
Equipment: walking boots, walking pole(s), sunhat, fleece, windproof, long trousers, rain-

gear, picnic, plenty of water, swimwear
Access: 🚗 or 🚌 to/from Hermigua (Timetable 12); journey time from San Sebastián 35min. Alight at the bus stop near the DISA petrol station, 2.8km north of the church, or park nearby (28° 10.372'N, 17° 11.305'W).

This is a good walk for those who like a long hike but don't want to watch where they are putting their feet all the time. Almost all on tracks and lanes, it's easily followed but full of views both near and far-off.

Setting out from the BUS STOP/CAR PARK (❍) just north of the DISA PETROL STATION in **Hermigua**, follow notes for Walk 36 on page 117 to the CALHETA JUNCTION (❶; **40min**), then keep ahead on the lane down to **Playa de la Caleta** (❼). Swimming is safe here when the sea is calm.

Ten minutes back up the lane, you'll see a farm building with well-tended VINEYARDS on the far side of the *barranco*. About 80m further up the lane, turn left down a STEPPED PATH by a WALKERS' SIGNBOARD (❽), into the lushly cultivated valley floor. Cross the stream bed (**Barranco de Montoro**), climb into some terraced plots and turn left after 25m (GREEN/WHITE WAYMARKS). Ignore a fork off to the right and round the hillside. At a fork where a path goes left to Punta San Lorenzo (**1h50min**), keep right. Ten minutes later you round a nose of hillside and descend across a palm-filled stream bed, the **Cañada de Barraca**. Several minutes up a rocky ridge on the far side, fork left at a junction.
When you join a track near the farmstead of **El Palmar** (❾; **2h10min**), yappy dogs may appear. *(From here you could take a straightforward detour to Tagu-*

luche — allow an extra hour: just follow the track from El Palmar and, when you reach the main track, keep left for Taguluche. Returning, keep straight along the main track — the left fork.)
To make for Hermigua however, continue up the track alongside the farmstead, then *leave it* almost immediately past a stone and tile-roofed building,

Signposted walks like this one should be maintained by the island government and the routes highlighted on the Cabildo map recommended on page 34.

ascending a path to the right (in front of a big rock with white lettering: 'PALMAR'). A few minutes uphill you rejoin the main track just past an isolated farmstead and below a house. Turning right, follow it all the way back to the CALHETA JUNCTION (❶), then turn sharp left and retrace your steps to **Hermigua** (❍; **4h15min**).

119

Walk 38: PUNTA SAN LORENZO

Distance: 5.6km/3.5mi; 2h
Grade: ● quite easy; ups/downs of 270m/885ft; wide paths
Equipment: trainers, sunhat,

fleece, windproof, raingear, picnic, water, swimwear
Access: 🚌 park above a walkers' signboard 1.5km along the *(quite narrow, vertiginous)* road to Playa de la Caleta, on a hairpin bend by well-kept terraces (28° 10.299'N, 17° 10.321'W). If there is no room, park at the end of the road, above the beach. Nearest bus access is Hermigua: see Walks 36, 37; add 2h return.

T his little gem of a coastal walk, suitable for all ages, follows a wide, well-protected path below steep cliffs. The walk is at its best on a clear but breezy day, when the white horses are pounding the rocks. Exhilarating!

View down over Playa de la Caleta

Start out at the WALKERS' SIGN-BOARD (**○**) on the road to Playa de la Caleta. Walk down the STEPPED PATH into the well planted valley floor, past emerald terraces liberally sprinkled with palms. You may well be of some interest to a huge scarecrow on the far side of the **Barranco de Montoro**. Rising on the far side of the stream bed, turn left after just 25m, following the GREEN/WHITE WAYMARKS. Ignore a fork off to the right (to El Moralito; **❶**) and round the hillside, contouring.
The path comes to a VIEWPOINT on a crest straight above Playa de

la Caleta (**❷**; **12min**) and then turns right into a short side-*barranco*. Cross the stream bed and climb out the other side, to be met by more stunning views of the wild coastline. When the path forks some 150m beyond the stream crossing, keep left for 'LAS SALINAS'. The well protected path eventually rounds **Punta San Lorenzo** and ends above the remains of an OLD QUAY and the ruins of the 'DISPATCH OFFICE' (**❹**; **1h**).
(An English firm built the road to the beach and on to this quay in the late 19th century, with the plan of shipping tomatoes and bananas to Europe: a large crane once stood on the quay. But the project proved completely impractical, because whether carried on men's shoulders or by donkeys, there was no way to get enough produce to the quay to make it pay.)
Some rickety steps lead down to a small pool and a pebbly beach. Give them a miss if you're not sure-footed! *Only swim here when the sea is dead calm!* Return the same way to the WALKERS' SIGN-BOARD (**○**; **2h**).

Walk 39: EL CEDRO CIRCUIT FROM HERMIGUA

See also photographs on pages
87, 88 and 90
Distance: 10km/6.2mi;
4h20min
Grade: ●: very strenuous, with
an ascent/descent of 750m/
2460ft. You must be sure-footed
and have a head for heights.
Don't attempt in wet or windy
weather. Well signposted trails
(Trail 37, except for one stretch
on track)
Equipment: walking boots,
walking pole(s), sunhat, fleece,
windproof, gloves, long trousers,
raingear, picnic, water

Access: 🚗 or 🚐 to El Convento
— one of the upper districts
(*barrios*) in Hermigua, by the
plaza and church. Park about
50m north of this plaza, at a car
park on the west side of the road
(28° 9.177'N, 17° 11.925'W). At the
end of the hike you will have a
tiring uphill walk (100m/325ft)
along the main GM1 back to
your car — or you *could* take a
bus! Bus users (Timetable 12)
can alight at El Convento and
pick up the return bus just where
the hike ends; journey time
from/to San Sebastián 35min.

Following a watercourse, you head into the depths of
the Monteforte and Cedro *barrancos,* where sheer-
sided walls, lavishly draped in vegetation, tower above
you. Scaling these walls, and passing the islands highest
and largest waterfall, you stumble upon a sprinkling of
cottages at El Cedro, set at the edge of the laurel forest.
Homeward bound, a tranquil forestry track lures you
down a wooded crest … to your steep and rocky descent
path, from where you'll have a superb panorama over the
Hermigua valley. The circuit makes an ideal day out for
motorists just itching to pull on their boots.

Start out on the main road at **El
Convento**. Cross the road from
the bus stop near the PLAZA and
the CHURCH and take the
concrete steps 10m to the left
(○; sign on the wall, 'EL
CEDRO'/TRAIL 37). You climb
steeply up to a road in the *barrio*
of **San Pedro** (**5min**). Turn
right up this road, heading
below dramatic **Roque de San
Pedro**, pointing straight up out
of the *barranco* wall. (There are
in fact *two* rocks here, and they
are often called 'Los Gemelos',
The Twins — or 'Los Enamora-
dos', The Lovers.)
In about 10 minutes the trail
takes you left, off the road and
over a bridge, to walk along the
left-hand side of the **Barranco
de Monteforte**. Ignore two sets

of steps on your left and in just a few minutes re-cross to the right-hand side. Now, immersed in banana plantations and garden plots, the straightforward route heads up the valley, for much of the time in the company of a WATER PIPE.

Ascending stone-paved steps, the path eventually crosses to the left-hand side of the *barranco* and

climbs above a large WATER TANK (❶). The way narrows to no more than a passage, and soon you can see the end — a half-moon cliff-face with a fine veil of water trickling over it. Steps take you up and around the right-hand side of a DAM WALL (**Embalse de los Tiles**; ❷; **1h**). Continue on the trail 100m past the dam, zigzagging up the

The terraces of Monteforte

El Cedro (Walks 23, 24 and 39). Walk 24 is the best way to see this charming little community, if you don't have the time or stamina for a long hike.

Your descent to Hermigua has begun. You head down the neck of a ridge and rejoin the track. A minute later, the track fizzles out into a path, perhaps a bit over-grown. Rounding a ridge, you look straight down the valley as it opens out to the sea. Soon you join an old cobbled trail. Pass to the right of a derelict FARM BUILDING (**3h25min**), magnificently perched over-looking the valley. Step down through abandoned terraces. Crossing a *barranco*, keep straight on round the hillside and pass below a WATER TANK on the top of the ridge. When you come to the **Ermita de San Juan** (❽; **3h55min**), take time to soak up another superb view down the valley.

Coming back from the chapel, you *could* follow the lane ahead to start back to El Convento — see the map and allow about an hour. But the main walk keeps to the trail: descend the steps to the left just at the end of the lane. A little over 10 minutes below the chapel, pass some houses and join a road. Cross it, walk along to the left for a few metres/yards, then descend steps. At the next road crossing, your continuing steps are a few metres/yards to the right. Squeeze past rustic cottages and down to the MAIN ROAD (❾; **4h20min**) in **Hermigua** by the ETHNOGRAPHIC MUSEUM (BUS STOP). If you've left a car at El Convento, walk up the main road to fetch it — about 650m/half a mile, with an extra 100m/330ft of ascent... or take the bus!

right-hand wall of the *barranco* to a pass. This ascent is awesome — affording a wonderful VIEW (❸) back down over the Hermigua valley and the Roque San Pedro, as well as to the **Boca del Chorro**, the highest water-fall on the island.

An ELECTRICITY PYLON marks the PASS at the top of the valley (❹; **1h45min**), from where you look straight onto **El Cedro**, a hand-ful of houses set in an untidy cultivated basin, embraced by the laurel forest. Following the stream bed, you arrive at a CAMPING AREA and the popular BAR/RESTAURANT LA VISTA (❺) just above it.

From the car park above LA VISTA, follow the steep road climbing to the right. At a junction, pick up a wide path ascending the bank on the right (above a greyish-coloured house, the CASA RURAL EL REFUGIO). A minute later, take another path on the right. Still climbing, you enter a cool dense forest, steeped in moss and lichen. Meeting a FORESTRY TRACK (❻; **2h30min**), turn right downhill. After about 35 minutes of descent, turn sharp right on another track. But just 35m after turning off, take a SIGNPOSTED PATH (❼) down to the right.

Walk 40: FROM AGULO TO VALLEHERMOSO

Note: The Garajonay Park Visitors' Centre (Juego de Bolas) is open daily from 09.30-16.30.

Distance: 14.4km/9mi; 4h25min

Grade: ●❗ strenuous, with ascents/descents of 750m/2000ft overall. Beyond El Teón, the descent is steep and gravelly; you must be sure-footed and have a head for heights. Don't attempt in wet or windy weather.

Equipment: walking boots, walking pole(s), sunhat, fleece, wind/rainproofs, long trousers, picnic, plenty of water

Access: 🚐 or 🚗 to the Agulo bus stop on the GM1 at the edge of the village (Timetable 12); journey time from San Sebastián 50min. Park by the bus stop (28° 11.155'N, 17° 11.663'W). Return on 🚐 from Vallehermoso bus station (Timetable 12); journey time to San Sebastián 1h25min, or to Agulo for your car (35min)

Short walk 1: From Agulo to Las Rosas (7.3km/4.5mi; 2h 30min). ● Fairly strenuous, with an overall ascent of 600m/2000ft. Equipment and access as main walk. Follow the main walk to ❺ (2h15min), then cross the road and go straight down a lane through Las Rosas and on to the main road. The bus stop (ⓐ; Vallehermoso 🚐, as above) is at the junction.

Short walk 2: From Las Rosas to Vallehermoso (8.3km/5.1mi; 1h50min). ●❗ Easy, except for the short but steep descent of about 100m/330ft beyond El Teón; overall ascent 200m/650ft. You must be sure-footed and have a head for heights, and don't attempt in wet or windy weather. Equipment as main walk. Access: 🚐 to Las Rosas (Vallehermoso bus, Timetable 12); the stop (ⓐ) is just past the turn-off to La Palmita. Follow the lane from the bus stop up to the Amalahuigue Reservoir (❺), then use the notes for the main walk from the 2h15min-point to the end. Return as main walk.

You'll remember this walk for its enchanting valleys. The first, finely etched into the landscape, leaves a deep impression — both figuratively and literally. You climb into scrub-daubed hills, dotted with dwellings. Approaching the tree-line, settlement thins and, from the top of a crest, you overlook an immense cauldron of cascading ridges. In their midst sits Vallehermoso. A most rewarding descent follows, as you drop into a plunging valley drenched with palms, its high rock walls flecked with pines. Here the terraced plots are a work of art; you have the feeling you could stroll in this valley forever.

Off the bus on the GM1 in **Agulo** (⚪), **start off** by heading up the ROAD TOWARDS VALLE-HERMOSO, then — virtually immediately — take the first right turn into a cobbled street. Follow this straight through Agulo, ignoring all side-streets. At a T-junction after 150m, turn right, after another 250m passing the pretty village square with its domed CHURCH and old houses with high latticed windows. Keep the church on your right and continue on a cobbled lane, ignoring turn-offs. You can see the cemetery off to the right in the distance, and you will no doubt spot some RED/WHITE WAYMARKS of the **GR 132** on street furniture. Banana groves sever the three separate *barrios* (districts) that make up the village.

At another T-junction turn right towards the CEMETERY (❶). Then, just 25m beyond it, climb a cobbled trail half-left up the hillside (RED/WHITE WAYMARKS,

Descending through El Teón

WOODEN FENCING). Tenerife sits just across the sea, a vista of which Agulo is justly proud. On reaching the VALLEHERMOSO ROAD again (**20min**), turn right

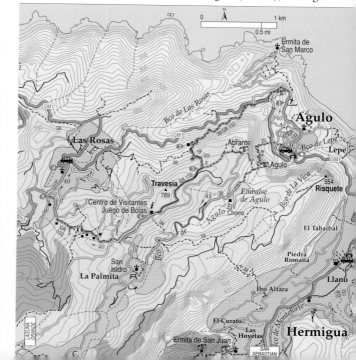

and walk about 50m uphill, to find your continuing trail on the left. You head steeply uphill on cobbles (ignore the minor branch-off to the left).

At a junction about 35 minutes from the road, just beyond a CHARMING OLD HOUSE (❷) with verandas, your trail (still the GR 132) turns abruptly up to the left towards the JUEGO DE BOLAS. Mounting the crest of the ridge, the path follows a deeply-eroded watercourse and crosses a ridge soaked in rich volcanic hues. (*Note:* 10 minutes down the crest of this ridge is the **Mirador de Abrante** overlooking Agulo. The time for this detour has *not* been included in the main walk.) Follow the **GR 132** past the TURN-OFF TO THE MIRADOR (❸), to a wide path/track just *over* the crest. Turn right uphill here. A sweeping view up the Barranco de Agulo follows. Joining a road, you come to the **Centro de Visitantes Juego de Bolas** (❹; **1h35min**). There's a fine garden with native plants, handicraft displays, and an informative film devoted to the Garajonay National Park.

From here set off up the adjoining LAGUNA GRANDE ROAD. A few minutes beyond the turn-off to La Palmita and Aceviños, turn right downhill with the **GR 132** on a trail (FINGERPOST: 'LAS ROSAS'). A minute along, cross a road and continue down into a tributary valley of the Las Rosas *barranco*. The trail passes to the right of a chained off private property, crosses a stream bed and climbs straight up the other side. It runs between a couple of houses, crosses the end of a track and then rises alongside an enclosed, abandoned vineyard on the left. After five minutes' ascent, on the top of the crest, the path reaches

some buildings (almost hidden by vegetation). Just before the buildings, at a Y-fork, keep right on a path alongside a small WATER PIPE. Continuing to the right, you emerge on another crest and pass above two POWER PYLONS. This is the edge of the heather belt bordering the laurel forest.

The trail continues left round the hillside, passes another PYLON on the next crest and drops down over the crest. Joining another path, turn right, descending steeply to an access road. Follow this downhill; then, just past the last house on the crest, descend concrete steps on the left to another road and the **Amalahuigue Reservoir** (❺; **2h15min**). *(Short walk 1 heads down to Las Rosas here, and Short walk 2 joins here.)*

Crossing the reservoir wall, you look down into Las Rosas. At the end of the wall, go left on the road, ignoring several side-roads and tracks. As you circle the top of the valley, a road and then a track (the **GR 132**) join from the right. Keeping to the road, after about 250m you reach a *mirador* at **Rosa de las Piedras** (❻; **2h55min**), with a view across an immense *caldera* filled with cascading ridges and glowing-green vegetable plots. Next to it is the friendly restaurant Roque Blanco with great views as well as good food — a pleasant place for a refreshment break. Follow the road past the *mirador*, ignoring three roads to the left. The road heads right and descends into the valley, hugging the sheer hillside. Ignore all side roads as you wind downhill.

At the end of the road, barely 15 minutes down, descend a few steep steps and continue on a narrow path. You drop down to terraces and cut across them to the stone houses of **El Teón**, balancing on a narrow ridge high in the valley. You meet a FORK (**7**) here: keep right on the steep gravelly path straight down this sheer-sided ridge (inexperienced walkers may find the first few minutes unnerving). You have a good view of **Roque El Cano**, a landmark for all walks around Vallehermoso. On meeting a TRACK (**3h40min**), follow it downhill into the setting shown below. Around 35 minutes down (five minutes after the way becomes tarred for the second time), turn left on a path. When you rejoin the road, follow it downhill to the MAIN ROAD in **Vallehermoso**. Turn left uphill to the ROUNDABOUT, then follow the GM1 towards 'VALLE GRAN REY'. The BUS STATION is 250m along this road, on your right (**8**; **4h25min**).

Roque El Cano rises above the 'valley of 1001 palms' at Vallehermoso, the highlight of this walk.

Walk 41: CIRCUIT FROM AGULO TO THE CENTRO DE VISITANTES AND MIRADOR DE ABRANTE

Note: The Garajonay Park Visitors' Centre (Juego de Bolas) is open daily from 09.30-16.30.
Distance: 12km/7.5mi; 4h05min
Grade: ●‼ fairly strenuous, with ascents/descents of 600m/ 2970ft overall. You must be sure-footed and have a head for heights. Don't attempt in wet or windy weather. Well signposted trails
Equipment: walking boots, walking pole(s), sunhat, fleece, wind/rainproofs, long trousers, picnic, plenty of water

Access: 🚌 or 🚗 to/from the Agulo bus stop on the GM1 at the edge of the village (Time-table 12); journey time from San Sebastián 50min. Ample parking by the bus stop (28° 11.155'N, 17° 11.663'W).
Short walk: Mirador de Abrante (3.5km/2mi; 55min).
● Fairly easy, with a descent/ ascent of 100m/330ft. Trainers will suffice. Access by 🚗: park at the Centro de Visitantes (Car tour 6). Use notes from the 2h-point in the main walk at ❹; return the same way.

Agulo is the most spectacularly sited village on the island, and this walk is one long *mirador*. It takes you up two two viewpoints from where you can appreciate the village setting, before returning to Agulo above the pretty Barranco de las Rosas. Midway, be sure to call in at the Visitors' Centre for enlightenment.

Start the walk in **Agulo**: from the BUS STOP (⊙) follow the MAIN ROAD TOWARDS VALLEHER-MOSO, past the POST OFFICE. A minute along, just past the PHARMACY, turn right up stone steps (FINGERPOST: 'ROUTES 34, 35; MIRADOR DE ABRANTE, CENTRO DE VISITANTES', and others). Rise through terracing, cross a lane and, a minute later, cross the main road. The trail heads steeply up towards the base of the cliffs and then, with-out respite, climbs in zigzags to a pass at the **Mirador de Agulo** (❶; **45min**), from where you can marvel at the village setting, the terracing, banana plantations, the tunnel under its sugarloaf guardian ... and El Teide on Tenerife.
From here the route swings right, away from the Barranco de Lepe, to ascend above the **Embalse de Agulo**. On reaching a tarred lane, follow it up the

valley; two minutes later, just above the Casas del Chorro holiday complex, turn left on a road which later becomes a track.
Fifteen minute from the dam, the track crosses to the left-hand side of the stream; five minutes later ignore a SHORT-CUT to the Visitors' Centre via a bridge on the right (❷; Trail 34). From here the way is tarred, then stone-laid. Two minutes later you cross a small ravine. Some 550m further on — 50m past a turning place — turn right uphill. At a junction three min-utes up, turn right and climb to the **San Isidro** chapel and PICNIC SITE at **La Palmita** (❸; **1h40min**). Now ascend to the Aceviños/El Cedro road, and turn right to the excellent Gara-jonay Visitors' Centre (**Juego de Bolas**; ❹; **2h**).
Leaving, take the road between the centre and now-closed Bar-

Agulo is the most superbly sited village on the island, and where better to appreciate the setting than from the Mirador de Abrante's glass 'skywalk', especially at sunrise

Restaurant TAMBOR (RED/WHITE WAYMARKED **GR 132**). After 100m, continue straight ahead on a washed-out red earthen track. About 15 minutes from the Visitors' Centre, past a small pine wood, turn half left up a minor track at a Y-FORK (**5**). Just 125m further on, at ANOTHER Y-FORK (**6**), is your ongoing route back to Agulo. But first, continue straight ahead down the crest for under 10 minutes, to the **Mirador de Abrante** (**7**; **2h25min**) — a spectacular viewpoint with a GLASS SKYWALK over the enormous drop above Agulo and a welcoming bar-café (which has no doubt contributed to the demise of the Tambor restaurant).

Back at the turn-off for Agulo, turn right; the path follows a greyish erosion gully. Soon you're on a cobbled trail, with fine views over the Barranco de Las Rosas. When the trail forks above a CHARMING OLD HOUSE (**8**), turn right with the **GR 132**. When you eventually meet the main road, follow it to the right for 50m, then turn left back onto the trail. Rounding a nose of rock, you descend to the village CEMETERY (**9**), from where a cobbled road leads back to the BUS STOP at **Agulo** (**○**; **4h05min**).

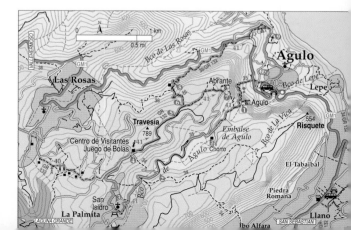

Walk 42: LA MESETA CIRCUIT FROM VALLEHERMOSO

Distance: 14km/8.7mi; 4h40min

Grade: ●❗: strenuous, with an ascent of 600m/2000ft at the outset (overall ascent 700m). You must be sure-footed and have a head for heights. The path up to La Meseta (GR 131) is sometimes overgrown, and in places narrow, steep and slippery underfoot. Don't attempt in wet weather. Good signposting: the walk partly follows the GR 131 and GR 132, also Trail 5

Equipment: walking boots, walking pole(s), sunhat, fleece, windproof, long trousers, long-sleeved shirt, raingear, picnic, plenty of water

Access: 🚗 or 🚌 to/from Vallehermoso. Park in the village, in the car park by the roundabout (28° 10.740'N, 17° 15.959'W); or bus to the station (Timetables 12, 14, 15); journey time from San Sebastián 1h25min

Alternative walk 1: Presa de los Gallos (12.8km/8mi; 2h40min return). ● Easy, gentle descent/ascent of 200m/650ft. Access by 🚗 or 🚌 to/from a parking area for the Chorros de Epina (29° 9.844'N, 17° 17.835'W). From there walk south along the road, then turn left on signposted **Trail 5** opposite the lane to the Chorros. When this trail meets the Meseta forestry track, follow it to where it ends at the small reservoir (**7**); you skirt the

A small reservoir below the Camino Forestal de la Meseta; Alternative walk 1 visits a similar reservoir.

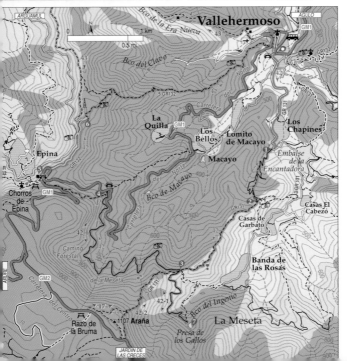

laurel forest, with fine views over the impressive valleys surrounding Vallehermoso and with a host of bright flowers in spring.
Alternative walk 2: From Las Hayas to Vallehermoso (9km/ 5.6mi; 2h50min). ● Easy-moderate, with a descent of 800m/2625ft; equipment as main walk. Access: 🚌 or 🚐 to Las Hayas (Timetables 11, 14, 16); return by taxi from Valle-hermoso — to your base or your car. To begin, follow WALK 16 on page 75 to the **Jardín de las Creces** PICNIC AREA. Then, instead of turning left, keep

ahead on the forestry road (**GR 131**) signed 'CARRETERA DORSAL'. When you meet the main GM2 road, turn left. After 100m turn right on TRAIL 3, signposted to 'VALLEHERMOSO'. This some-times steep path (still also the red/white waymarked **GR 131**) takes you down to the CAMINO FORESTAL DE LA MESETA (**3**; 1h25min). *Either* cross straight over and follow the **GR 131** all the way to the ROUNDABOUT (**○**) in **Vallehermoso** (9km) *or* turn left and follow the main walk from the 1h45min-point (14km, moderate-strenuous; 4h40min).

This walk circles what looks like a great crater with hundreds of valleys etched into it. The La Meseta forestry track, which runs along the fringe of the laurel forest, provides a pleasant interlude in this otherwise harsh, rocky terrain.

Set out by leaving **Valleher-moso** on the road branching south off the ROUNDABOUT (**○**), past the BAR AMAYA on the plaza and the POST OFFICE (Calle Triana, the **GR 131**). Turn right at the T-junction. The GR 131 splits 30m further on: ignore the signposted branch to the left and continue up the road into the **Barranco del Valle**. You wind above banana plots and vege-table gardens. After 1.6km, just where the road curves sharply left (towards the Embalse de la Encantadora, not visible from this point; **25min**), take the first track on the right (**❶**; still the red/white waymarked **GR 131**, signposted 'LA MESETA'), cutting up into a narrow *barranco*. A gully runs below on your right. Some 100m from the start of the track, go through a chain barrier.
After 15 minutes, just after rounding the end of the ridge, climb a path up to the right. Ascending a steep ridge, you'll

be brushing through rock-roses. Meeting the track again, cross straight over. The next time you meet the track, you can either cross straight over again or take a path 80m further uphill. Reaching the top of a crest (**1h**), a view unfolds down into another cultivated valley, the **Barranco del Ingenio**.
Turn right for 'LA MESETA' (**❷**) at this junction, climbing on or near the top of the crest all the way up. It's steep. Roque El Cano (photograph page 127) is the enormous rock that disrupts the landscape behind you. A corner of Vallehermoso comes into view, with its *barranco* and, on the far side of the ridge, you look down onto small clusters of homesteads in the Barranco del Ingenio. Nearing **La Meseta**, the path is steeper, narrow in places, sometimes overgrown and skiddy underfoot.
Joining the CAMINO FORESTAL DE LA MESETA (**3**; 1h45min), turn right. *(Alternative walk 2 joins*

here, via the path opposite, and the Presa de los Gallos, goal of Alternative walk 1, lies 20 minutes to the left.) The track skirts the edge of the forest with some pretty wooded spots.

Just before reaching the MAIN ROAD, turn left on signposted **Trail 5** (④), a path that runs parallel to the road, gently rising and falling for about 20 minutes. You emerge opposite a cobbled lane to the **Chorros de Epina** PICNIC AREA/SPRINGS. Visit the springs (or not), then follow the road to the right, past the popular eponymous RESTAURANT (⑤), before turning left on a road to 'TAGULUCHE/ALOJERA' (**3h05min**).

Ten minutes along, on a hairpin bend, you will climb the small road on the right, up towards a large MAST (the **GR 132**). But first make a detour 100m along to the *left,* to enjoy the VIEW: the group of houses in the sheltered flat valley below, surrounded by hills, is the hamlet of Tazo. On clear days the twin humps of La Palma appear above the clouds.

Return to the junction and head up the narrow road towards the mast. Three minutes up, turn right downhill on an earthen track (⑥; still the red/white way-marked GR 132). Three minutes along, take the trail branching off to the right. With views out across a massive depression of ridges and valleys and over the Embalse de la Encantadora to the right of Vallehermoso, this GR trail takes you all the way to the town. When you're directly above it, there's another superb VIEW (**4h20min**) down the Barranco del Valle to the sea. A little over five minutes later, from the first house, a concrete path takes you back down to the centre of **Vallehermoso** (○; **4h40min**).

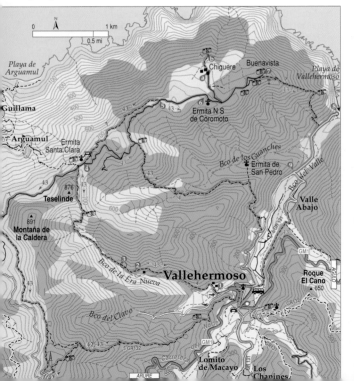

Walk 43: CIRCUIT FROM VALLEHERMOSO TO THE ERMITA SANTA CLARA AND PLAYA DE VALLEHERMOSO

See map opposite
Distance: 13km/8mi; 4h30min
Grade: ●❗ strenuous; ascents/
descents of 750m/2460ft overall.
You must be sure-footed and
have a head for heights on the
descent to Playa de Vallehermoso
— it is very steep and gravelly,
*not recommended for inexperienced
walkers*. Don't attempt this
descent in wet or windy weather.
All on well signposted trails
Equipment: walking boots,
walking pole(s), sunhat, fleece,
windproof, long trousers, raingear, picnic, water; swimwear in
summer, when the pool is filled
— the sea is far too dangerous!
Access: ⛐ or ⛍ to/from Vallehermoso. Park in the village, in
the car park by the roundabout
(28° 10.740'N, 17° 15.959'W); or bus
to the station (Timetables 12,
14, 15); journey time from San
Sebastián 1h25min
Shorter walk: Out-and-back to
the Ermita Santa Clara (9km/
5.6mi; 3h20min). ● Strenuous,
with an ascent/descent of 630m/
2065ft. Not recommended in
wet weather. Equipment, access
as main walk. Follow main walk
to the **Santa Clara chapel** (④;

1h50min) and return the same
way — or on signposted Trail 4
(add 2km; 35min).
*Alternative walk: Ermita de
Santa Clara circuit with return
via the GR 132* (13.4km/8.3mi;
4h40min). ● Access, equipment, grade as Short walk. This
circuit avoids the steep and
gravelly descent to Playa de
Vallehermoso; instead there is a
gentle descent through laurel
forest. Follow the main walk up
to the **Ermita de Santa Clara**
(④; 1h50min). Now turn *left*
on the track, away from the
ermita. If there is no fog, you
look down on two small settlements at the end of the world —
Tazo and Arguamul. Some
20min along, take a track
forking left. This becomes a
SIGNPOSTED PATH running
parallel with the track over to the
right. Alojera comes into view
and the massive cliffs behind it.
On the horizon are the crests
traversed in Walks 11-14. Walk
past a LARGE MAST (3h05min)
for 250m, then pick up Walk 42
at (⑥; see the last paragraph
opposite) to get back to Vallehermoso (○; 4h40min).

Reaching Vallehermoso is an expedition in itself.
Whether travelling by car or by bus you crawl over
a mountainous relief carved out with plunging ravines,
which leave a skeleton of fine-lined ridges tapering off into
the sea. Each unfolding view is better than the last. This
exhilarating descent by switchback road is breathtaking!
The walk itself gives you commanding panoramas of the
normally inaccessible north coast and beyond — on clear
days as far as Tenerife and her showpiece, El Teide.

Start out from the ROUNDABOUT
(○) in Vallehermoso: climb the
narrow street at the right of the
BAR CENTRAL (CALLE MAYOR).
Passing above the CHURCH, join
the VALLE GRAN REY ROAD and
follow it left uphill as far as the

first bend. Here take the first
road on the right, to the
CEMETERY (①). Then take the old
signposted trail on the right-
hand side of the cemetery and
descend into the floor of the
barranco. Cross a footbridge and

turn right, to climb towards a couple of houses on the hillside. Roque El Cano (photograph page 127), an enormous spearhead of rock overshadowing the village, commands your attention as you climb.

Keep left at the fork just below the houses. Brushing against the last house, curve round to head up into the **Barranco de la Era Nueva**. The hillsides are freckled with *sabina,* an indigenous juniper. Ignore all paths down to the left. You pass an isolated, abandoned house and then a small RESERVOIR (**❷**; **40min**). The trail then crosses an old circular THRESHING FLOOR (**❸**) and begins a series of stream bed crossings, amidst cane, *tabaiba,* brambles, ferns and aromatic *artemisia*. Falcons often hover overhead.

After crossing the stream bed for the last time, you enter the evergreen forest and the real ascent begins. Scaling the **Teselinde ridge**, your view expands to encompass the central spine of the island curling around this immense depression of valleys. A cape of dark cloud, pierced by the occasional ray of sunlight, usually rests on the *cumbre*. Entering heather, the way flattens out. A scattering of white houses in the distance reveals Tamagarda. The path edges its way along the top of the ravine for about 10 minutes, close to the tree line, until you reach a flat crest. If the mist hasn't enveloped you, you'll see the Ermita Santa Clara over to the right.

When you come to an earthen track, turn right and follow it to the **Ermita Santa Clara** (**❹**; **1h50min**). If the mist lifts, you'll have splendid views from here over the remote village of Arguamul and the group of

peaked rocks off its shore, as well as across to La Palma. *(The Shorter walk turns back here and the Alternative walk turns left on the track.)*

From here take the well-defined and protected ridgetop path to the left; you will rejoin the TRACK (**❺**) from the *ermita* a short way ahead. Some 30 minutes later, another chapel comes into sight, the **Ermita Nuestra Senora de Coromoto** (**❻**; **2h20min**), laid bare to the winds on an open crest. Passing it, you descend into a high valley. A rainbow of pastel pinks, browns, greys, mauves and yellows glows out of a bare hillside below. Over on the left, a few stray palms adorning a rocky ridge disclose **Chiguere** (**ⓐ**), which sits almost unnoticed against the rocks. Ignore the turn-off to this decayed settlement. (But for a truly spectacular view of Los Organos, *do* take the turn off to this old settlement and, once you reach the houses, cross the hilltop behind them and go on some 100m further, to the RIDGE (**ⓑ**), from where the whole structure of Los Organos is visible, from the sea to the top.)

Some 15 minutes later ignore a track to the right to a viewpoint on a hilltop; a minute after that you catch sight of the coast (**2h35min**), and a stunning seascape unfolds. Ridges, serrating the coastline, tumble off into a faintly-green sea. Vallehermoso comes out of hiding, trailing a valley lined with banana groves. The entire countryside is spotted with *sabina*. On your right here, you'll spot a sign indicating the start of the zigzagging path down to the beach. But first, for an even better view of the coast, continue along the track for another

100m, to the **Buenavista** *mirador* (**7**).

Returning to the sign, begin the descent in the setting shown below. After two minutes, the worst is behind you. *Always* keep your eyes on the path, although the views are irresistible! As well as *sabina*, you'll see a plethora of tubular-stemmed *Ceropegia ceratophora* growing on the slopes. Your view soon stretches all the way up the Barranco del Valle. Closer to the road, the way swings right, crosses a steep slope and joins a stream bed. Meeting the road, turn left downhill to **Playa de Vallehermoso** (**8**; **3h 35min**), described on page 30.

Then follow the road gently back uphill to the south for 1km and, just past a BUS SHELTER (**9**), turn left with the **GR 131** ('VALLEHERMOSO 2,6KM'), crossing the stream. As afternoon shadows creep across the ravine walls, you amble alongside a valley floor crammed with banana groves and cane; the stream bubbles away below you. The lane peters out into a path, and GR FINGERPOSTS lead you into town. You pass the BUS STATION and come back to the ROUNDABOUT in **Vallehermoso** (**○**; **4h30min**).

Coastal scenery near the 'Buenavista' viewpoint

Walk 44: PRESA DE MERIGA

Distance: 1.5km/1mi; 40min-1h
Grade: ● an easy stroll on forestry tracks, with just a little climbing up the valley to the reservoir (50m/150ft)

Equipment: trainers, warm clothing in cooling fog

Access: 🚗 to the Presa de Meriga (28° 9.243'N, 17° 14.199'W). From the Centro de Visitantes Juego de Bolas head south on the Laguna Grande road for 2.7km, then turn left at an inconspicuous wooden sign for 'Palmita'. After 1.4km *ignore* the sharp left turn to Meriga; keep ahead to a sign for 'Presa de Mériga'.

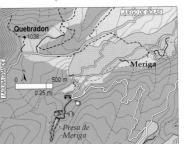

This short ramble, a perfect leg stretcher during Car tour 6, is *not* a good introduction to walking on La Gomera … it's almost flat! If you find many island walks too strenuous, then *do* look at page 8: our suggested picnic places will often take you to Gomera's most exquisite beauty spots after just a short stroll. This walk is an example. Note, however, that when we went to check the walk just before going to press with this edition, the reservoir was being rebuilt and out of bounds — so the walk may well be very different when you use this book!

Start out at the SIGN 'PRESA DE MERIGA' (**O**). Set off for the lake up the wide forestry track. After passing a VIEWPOINT (**1**) over the bowl of the *barranco*, fork left on the signposted path to the **Presa de Meriga**. Follow the path round the reservoir: it was flooded in the 1980s, and the skeletal tree trunks emerging from the bed of the lake create beautiful patterns and add to the mystical quality of the area — especially in fog!
When you come back to the DAM WALL, a track takes you back to the signpost and your car (**O**; **40min**).

❀ Appendix

Timetables of particular interest to walkers are found on the following pages. We have included as much information about the whole of Tenerife as possible in this book, but do remember that to explore the whole island *on foot*, you will need the companion volume, *Landscapes of Tenerife (Teno • Orotava • Anaga • Cañadas)*.

TOURIST INFORMATION

Both islands have very comprehensive websites, with good maps (including downloadable walking maps) and videos. For **Tenerife** go to www.webtenerife.co.uk; for **Gomera** log on to www.lagomera.travel. The islands' local tourist offices and visitors' centres are another excellent source of (free) information and maps.

BUS, PLANE AND FERRY TIMETABLES

Below is a list of destinations on Tenerife (T) and La Gomera (G) covered by the following timetables. Numbers following places names are *timetable* numbers. There are far more buses *and departures* on Tenerife than those listed here; complete **Tenerife timetables** can be viewed and downloaded from www.titsa.com (the island bus company, with web pages in English). **Gomera timetables** can be checked online at www.guaguagomera. com. Although the website is only in Spanish, just click on 'Horarios' — all the lines are shown, and it is very straightforward to compare times with those in this book to see if there are any changes.

Adeje (T) 5, 9
Agulo (G) 12
Alajeró (G) 13
Arona (T) 4, 6
Arure (G) 11, 16
Boca Tauce (T) 4
Casa de la Seda (G) 11, 16
Caseta de los Noruegos (G) 11
Chipude (G) 11, 14, 16
Cruce de la Zarcita (G) 11
Degollada de Peraza (G) 11, 13

Hermigua (G) 12
Imada turn-off (G) see Alajeró
Jerduñe (G) 13, 17
La Calera (G) 11, 16
La Escalona (T) 4, 7
Las Casetas (G) 12
Las Hayas (G) 11, 14, 16
Lomo Blanco (T) 4
Lomo del Balo (G) 11, 16
Los Cristianos (T) 2-4, 7-10, 18; see also car ferry timetables, page 133

Los Gigantes (T) 9
Los Granados (G) 11, 16
Pajarito (G) 11
Parador de las Cañadas (T) 4
Playa de las Américas (T) 2-4, 7-10
Playa de San Juan (T) 9
Playa de Santiago (G) 13, 17, 18
Puerto de la Cruz (T) 1, 2
Roque de Agando (G) 11

San Sebastián (G) 11-13; see also ferry timetables, page 138
Santa Cruz (T) 1, 3
Santiago del Teide (T) 8
Targa turn-off (G) 13, 16
Valle Gran Rey (G) 11, 16, 18
Vallehermoso (G) 12, 14, 15
Vilaflor (T) 4, 7
Vueltas (G) 11, 16, 18

BUS SERVICES — TENERIFE

1 🚌 102: Santa Cruz to Puerto de la Cruz; *express*; daily

Santa Cruz	La Laguna	Puerto	*Sat/Sun/holidays*
07.40	07.55	08.40	*The times shown at the*
then every 30 minutes at 10 and 40min past the hour until			*left are from Mon to Fri.*
21.00	21.45	22.00	*On Sat/Sun/holidays*
Puerto	La Laguna	Santa Cruz	*buses are almost as*
06.15	07.00	07.15	*frequent but they depart*
then every 30 minutes at 15 and 45min past the hour until			*at different minutes*
21.15	22.00	22.15	*past the hour.*

2 🚌 343: Costa Adeje to Puerto de la Cruz; *express*; daily

Costa Adeje	Los Cristianos	Puerto	Puerto	Los Cristianos	Costa Adeje
09.00	09.15	11.30	09.00	11.15	11.30
11.30	11.45	14.00	11.25	13.40	13.55
15.30	15.45	18.00	15.25	17.40	17.55
18.00	18.15	20.30	18.00	20.15	20.30

3 🚌 111: Santa Cruz to Costa Adeje; daily

Santa Cruz	La Candelaria	Poris de Abona	Los Cristianos	Costa Adeje
		Mondays to Fridays		
06.55	07.10	07.45	08.20	08.35
		and every 30minutes until		
20.25	20.40	21.15	21.50	22.05
		Saturdays, Sundays and holidays		
Departures from Santa Cruz at 07.05, 09.40, 12.40, 13.15, 15.55, 19.15				
Same intermediate and final journey times				

Costa Adeje	Los Cristianos	Poris de Abona	La Candelaria	Santa Cruz
		Mondays to Fridays		
06.55	07.10	07.45	08.20	08.35
		and every 30minutes until		
20.25	20.40	21.15	21.50	22.05
		Saturdays, Sundays and holidays		
Departures from Santa Cruz at 08.25, 11.20, 13.55, 14.35, 17.35, 20.45				
Same intermediate and final journey times				

4 🚌 342: Costa Adeje to Las Cañadas; daily

Costa Adeje station (depart)	09.15	El Portillo (depart)	15.15
Los Cristianos	09.30	**Visitors' Centre**	15.17
Arona	09.45	**Teide cable car**	15.40
Vilaflor	10.10	**Parador**	16.00
Boca Tauce	10.35	**Boca Tauce**	16.05
Parador	10.45	**Vilaflor**	16.25
Teide cable car	10.55	**Arona**	17.00
Visitors' Centre	11.43	**Los Cristianos**	17.30
El Portillo	11.45	**Costa Adeje station**	17.45

5 🚌 447: Los Cristianos to Adeje; daily

Los Cristianos	Playa Américas	Adeje	*Sat/Sun/holidays*
06.45	07.00	07.15	*The times shown at the*
and approximately every 30 minutes until			*left are from Mon to Fri.*
21.05	21.20	21.35	*On Sat/Sun/holidays*
Adeje	Playa Américas	Granadilla	*buses run hourly*
07.00	07.15	07.30	*anywhere from 10min*
and approximately every 30 minutes until			*to 45min past the hour.*
21.15	21.30	22.00	*Check the web for exact times.*

6 🚌 480: Los Cristianos to Arona; daily*

Los Cristianos	Arona		Arona	Los Cristianos
07.30	07.50		07.00	07.20
09.00	09.20		08.00	08.20
10.00	10.20		09.00	09.20
10.30	10.50		09.30	09.50
and approximately hourly until			and approximately hourly until	
19.30	19.50		20.00	20.20

*Check exact departure times on the web: some depart on the hour, others at 5min-30min past the hour; *Sat/Sun/holiday departures less frequent (only every 2-3 hours)*

7 🚌 482: Los Cristianos to Vilaflor; Sat/Sun/holidays *only*

Los Cristianos	La Escalona	Vilaflor
05.50	06.15	06.25
10.45	11.10	11.20
17.15	17.40	17.50

Vilaflor	La Escalona	Los Cristianos
06.30	06.40	07.05
11.30	11.40	12.05
18.00	18.10	18.35

8 🚌 460: Costa Adeje to Icod; daily

Costa Adeje	Guía de Isora	Santiago del Teide	Icod de los Vinos
07.45	08.10	08.35	09.10
09.50	10.15	10.40	11.15
11.45	12.10	12.35	13.10
14.10	14.35	15.00	15.35
16.05	16.30	16.55	17.30
18.25	18.50	19.15	19.50
20.00	20.25	20.50	21.25

Icod de los Vinos	Santiago del Teide	Guía de Isora	Costa Adeje
07.45	08.20	08.45	09.10
10.00	10.35	11.00	11.25
11.55	12.30	12.55	13.20
14.05	14.40	15.05	15.30
16.10	16.45	17.10	17.35
18.20	18.55	19.20	19.45
20.10	20.45	21.10	21.35

9 🚌 473: Los Cristianos to Los Gigantes; daily

Los Cristianos*	Adeje	Playa San Juan	Los Gigantes
06.45	07.15	07.40	08.05
07.15	07.45	08.10	08.35
	and every half hour until		
20.15	20.45	21.10	21.35
	then		
22.15	22.45	23.10	23.35

Los Gigantes	Playa San Juan	Adeje	Los Cristianos**
06.15	06.40	07.05	07.35
06.45	07.10	07.35	08.05
07.30	07.55	08.30	09.00
08.00	08.25	09.00	09.30
	and every half hour until		
21.00	21.25	22.00	22.30
	then		
21.20	21.45	22.20	22.50
21.40	22.05	22.40	23.10
22.30	22.55	23.20	23.45
23.30	23.55	01.20	01.45

Bus passes through Playa de las Américas *10 minutes later; **10 minutes earlier

10 🚌 111: Playa de las Américas — Aeropuerto del Sur; daily

Costa Adeje*	Aeropuerto	Aeropuerto	Costa Adeje**
06.00	06.40	07.00	07.40
	and every 30 minutes		
21.20	22.00	22.00	22.40

Passes through Los Cristianos *15 minutes later; **15 minutes earlier

BUS SERVICES — LA GOMERA

11 🚌 Línea 1: San Sebastián — Valle Gran Rey

San Sebastián	Degollada de Peraza	Cruce de la Zarcita	Pajarito	Chipude	Arure	Valle Gran Rey
10.30*	10.50*	10.55*	11.05*	11.20*	11.45*	12.20*
12.00#	12.20#	12.25#	12.35#	12.50#	13.15#	13.50#
15.30#	15.50#	15.55#	16.05#	16.20#	16.45#	17.20#
18.30#	18.50#	18.55#	19.05#	19.20#	19.45#	20.20#
20.30+	20.50+	20.55+	21.05+	21.20+	21.45+	22.20+
21.30=	21.50=	21.55=	22.05=	22.20=	22.45=	23.20=
21.45•	22.05•	22.10•	22.20•	22.35•	23.00•	23.35•

Valle Gran Rey	Arure	Chipude	Pajarito	Cruce de la Zarcita	Degollada de Peraza	San Sebastián
05.00#	05.35#	06.00#	06.15#	06.25#	06.30#	06.50#
08.00*	08.35*	09.00*	09.15*	09.25*	09.30*	09.50*
13.00#	13.05#	14.00#	14.15#	14.25#	14.30#	14.50#
14.30#	15.05#	15.30#	15.45#	15.55#	16.00#	16.20#
16.30•	17.05•	17.30•	17.45•	17.55•	18.00•	18.20•
18.00#	18.35#	19.00#	19.15#	19.25#	19.30#	19.50#

12 🚌 Línea 2: San Sebastián — Hermigua — Agulo — Vallehermoso

San Sebastián	Hermigua	Agulo	Las Rosas	Vallehermoso
10.30*	11.05*	11.20*	11.35*	11.55*
12.00#	12.35#	12.50#	13.05#	13.25#
15.30#	16.05#	16.55#	17.10#	17.30#
18.30#	19.05#	19.55#	20.10#	20.30#
20.30+	21.05+	21.55+	22.10+	22.30+
21.30=	22.05=	22.55=	23.10=	23.30=
21.45•	22.20•	23.10•	23.25•	23.45•

Vallehermoso	Las Rosas	Agulo	Hermigua	San Sebastián
05.30#	05.50#	06.05#	06.20#	06.55#
07.30+‡	07.50+‡	08.05+‡	08.20+‡	08.55+‡
08.00=•‡	08.20=•‡	08.35=•‡	08.50=•‡	09.25=•‡
13.30#‡	13.50#‡	14.05#‡	14.20#‡	14.55#‡
15.30#‡	15.50#‡	16.05#‡	16.20#‡	16.55#‡
17.00•	17.20•	17.35•	17.50•	18.25•
18.00#	18.20#	18.35#	18.50#	19.25#

13 🚌 Línea 3: San Sebastián — Playa de Santiago — Alajeró

San Sebastián	Peraza Pass	Playa Santiago	Alajeró	
07.00#‡	07.20#‡	07.45#‡	08.05#‡	Bus continues
10.30#‡	10.50#‡	11.15#‡	11.35#‡	to the turn-off
12.00#‡	12.20#‡	12.45#‡	13.05#‡	to Imada
15.30#‡	15.50#‡	16.15#‡	16.35#‡	
17.45#‡	18.05#‡	18.30#‡	18.50#‡	
20.30*‡	20.50*‡	21.15*‡	21.35*‡	
21.30=‡	21.50=‡	22.15=‡	22.35=‡	
21.45•‡	22.05•‡	22.30•‡	22.50√	

* daily (including holidays); = Sat; + Mon-Fri; # Mon-Sat; • Sun; ‡ connection to the airport

Alajeró	Playa Santiago	Peraza Pass	San Sebastián	
05.30#‡	05.45#‡	06.15#‡	06.35#‡	*Bus returns*
07.00*‡	07.15*‡	07.45*‡	08.05*‡	*from the turn-off*
13.30#‡	13.45#‡	14.15#‡	14.35#‡	*to Imada;*
15.30#‡	15.45#‡	16.15#‡	16.35#‡	*arrive early!*
17.30•‡	17.45•‡	18.15•‡	18.35•‡	
19.00#‡	19.15#‡	19.45#‡	20.05#‡	

14 🚌 Línea 4: Vallehermoso — Las Hayas — Chipude — La Dama

Departs **Vallehermoso** 06.30, 12.00 (a) *Mon-Fri only*
Departs **La Dama** 08.00 (a), 13.30 (a) *Mon-Fri only*
(a) connection to San Sebastián at Chipude via Línea 1

15 🚌 Línea 5: Vallehermoso — Epina — Alojera

Departs **Vallehermoso** 05.30, 13.30 *Mon-Fri only*
Departs **Alojera** 06.30 (a), 14.30 (a) *Mon-Fri only*
(a) connection to San Sebastián at Vallehermoso via Línea 2; connection to airport at San Sebastián via Línea 3 or Línea 7

16 🚌 Línea 6: Valle Gran Rey — Airport

Departs **Valle Gran Rey** *daily, two hours before flights*   ***bus may not run if flights are***
Departs **Airport** *daily, on arrival of flights*   ***cancelled! Call +34 922 14 11 01***

17 🚌 Línea 7: San Sebastián — Airport

Departs **San Sebastián** *daily, 1h45min before flights*   ***bus may not run if flights are***
Departs **Airport** *daily, on arrival of flights*   ***cancelled! Call +34 922 14 11 01***

18 ⛴ PASSENGER FERRY SERVICE — LA GOMERA

Fred Olsen (www.fredolsen.es) runs an express passenger ferry service between **San Sebastián** and **Valle Gran Rey** via **Playa Santiago**
Departs Valle Gran Rey for Playa de Santiago 06.30, 12.30, 17.00 *daily*
Departs Playa de Santiago for San Sebastián 07.20, 13.20, 17.50 *daily*
Departs San Sebastián for Playa de Santiago 10.45, 15.00, 21.00 *daily*
Departs Playa de Santiago for Valle Gran Rey 11.30, 15.40, 21.40 *daily*

INTER-ISLAND FLIGHTS

La Gomera can currently be reached by plane from Tenerife Norte or Gran Canaria; for information/reservations see www.bintercanarias.com.

INTER-ISLAND CAR FERRY SERVICES

Two companies operate car ferries between Los Cristianos on Tenerife and San Sebastián on Gomera. Ticket offices open about one hour before sailing time. Current timetables are shown below; update at the operators' websites.

Fred Olsen (www.fredolsen.es), Benchijigua Express: sailing time 50min
Departs Los Cristianos 09.30 *daily*, 12.30 *Mon-Thu & Sat*, 15.30 *Tue/Thu*, 16.00 *Sun*, 16.30 *Fri*, 19.00 *Tue/Thu/Sun*
Departs San Sebastián 08.00 *daily*, 11.00 *Mon-Thu & Sat*, 14.00 *Tue/Thu*, 15.00 *Fri*, 17.30 *Tue/Thu/Sat*, 18.00 *Mon/Wed/Fri/Sat*, 20.30 *Sun*

Naviera Armas (naviera-armas.com): sailing time 1h10min
Departs Los Cristianos 08.45 *daily*, 13.30 *Mon-Thu*, 16.30 *Fri*, 18.30 *Mon-Thu*, 17.45 *Sun*, 19.00 *Sat*, 21.00 *Sun*
Departs San Sebastián 07.00 *daily*, 11.00 *Mon-Fri*, 16.30 *Mon-Thu*, 17.00 *Sat*, 18.00 *Fri*, 19.15 *Sun*

Index

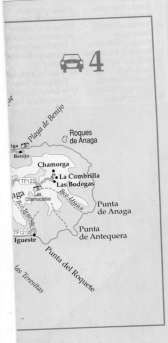

orway/Autobahn	
cipal road/Hauptstraße	
or road/Nebenstraße	
onal park/Nationalpark	
0 m (0-1300 ft)	
-800 m (1300-2600 ft)	
-2000 m (2600-6550 ft)	
0-3000 m (6550-9850 ft)	
/über 3000 m (9850 ft)	
of the car tour with ber/Gebiet der Autotour zugehöriger Nummer	
ation of the walk iet der Wanderung	

🛏	Isolated hotel
🛏	Isolated inn
△	Camping
✕	Isolated restaurant
⛽	Petrol station/Tankstelle
✝	Church.chapel/Kirche.Kapelle
★	Attraction/Sehenswürdigkeit
⊕	Medical centre/Klinik
⊓	Picnic tables/Picknicktische
📷	Viewpoint/Aussichtspunkt
🏰	Castle.Tower/Burg.Turm
✈	Airport/Flughafen
M	Museum
⤛	Trout farm/Forellenzucht
✿	Gardens/Gärten